Union Soldiers

—— *of* ——

Southwestern Illinois

John J. Dunphy

THE
History
PRESS

Published by The History Press
Charleston, SC
www.historypress.com

Copyright © 2024 by John J. Dunphy

First published 2024

Manufactured in the United States

ISBN 9781467156806

Library of Congress Control Number: 2023950633

Notice: The information in this book is true and complete to the best of our knowledge. It is offered without guarantee on the part of the author or The History Press. The author and The History Press disclaim all liability in connection with the use of this book.

For Loretta.

CONTENTS

ACKNOWLEDGMENTS

All photographs were taken by the author unless otherwise noted. Lacy Spraggins McDonald of Alton's Hayner Public Library was always willing to assist me in my research. David Scott shared his ancestor's Civil War memoir with me, which contributed so much to this book. My thanks to Davis Duffey, park guide at Andersonville National Historic Site, who searched for "the cowardly Major Birch" mentioned by Andrew Rodgers during his newspaper interview. The Madison County Historical Society should be commended for preserving several firsthand accounts by Union soldiers, including the handwritten memoir of William R. Eddington. A special thank-you goes to Jason D. Stratman of the Missouri Historical Society Library for providing me with information about the men of Company B of the 1st Missouri Volunteer Cavalry.

I hope that this new book meets with your approval, Pillie. Years ago, when you said how much you like to read, I knew we'd be friends.

INTRODUCTION

Few regions of the United States were stronger in their support of the Union during the Civil War than southwestern Illinois. Even its colleges rallied to the Federal banner. The entire graduating class of Shurtleff College in 1864 enlisted in the Union army. Shurtleff alumni proudly served in the Northern armies. This small Baptist college provided the Union with three generals: John Pope, John Cook and John Palmer. Appointed by Lincoln as military commander of the Department of Kentucky, Palmer played a critical role in ending slavery in the Bluegrass State. Shurtleff graduate Franklin Moore raised an independent cavalry regiment that he named the Madison County Rangers, which later became Company D of the 2nd Illinois Cavalry. McKendree College, located in Lebanon, rivaled Shurtleff in its support for the Union. Risdon Moore, a professor at the college who was acquainted with Lincoln, commanded the Illinois 117th Infantry, which included so many McKendree men that it became known as the "McKendree Regiment."

At least one hundred Black men from Madison County enlisted in the 29th Colored Infantry. These men knew the risks they were taking by volunteering to fight for the Union. The Confederacy had decreed that any Black man taken prisoner could be executed or sold as a slave, even if he had been born a free man. Lewis Martin, an escaped slave who had made his way to Upper Alton, enlisted in the 29th. He lost his left foot and right arm during the Battle of the Crater but still managed to avoid capture.

John Hale Sr. of Alton served in the Illinois 7th Infantry, which made history as the only regiment in the entire Union army to purchase its own guns—Henry rifles, an early repeating firearm capable of firing sixteen rounds before reloading was necessary. Such a formidable weapon gave

Hale and the other men of the 7th a tremendous advantage when facing enemy troops armed only with single-shot, muzzle-loading muskets that had a rate of fire of just three rounds per minute at best.

Bunker Hill, a small town in southern Macoupin County, has one of the most impressive statues of Abraham Lincoln in the United States. It was dedicated in 1904 to honor the men of that vicinity who enlisted in Company B of the 1st Missouri to fight for the Union.

This region's Union men who were captured by Rebel forces experienced the living hell of Confederate prisons. John T. King and Joseph Weeks survived incarceration in Georgia's Andersonville, while Andrew Rodgers was imprisoned in Virginia's Libby. George Uzzell was taken to Camp Ford in Texas, which was the largest Confederate prison west of the Mississippi.

European immigrants who settled in southwestern Illinois proved their loyalty to our nation by enlisting in the Union army. Swiss-born John Kuhn joined the Alton Jaegers, an Alton-based military unit in 1855. He had risen to the rank of captain when the Jaegers became Company A of the 9th Illinois Volunteer Infantry. He was later promoted to major. Kuhn distinguished himself in battle and struck a blow against slavery when he allowed a Black woman fleeing her master to seek refuge with the Illinois 9th. "The woman," an eyewitness account states, "came into Decatur with our Regiment" and "was so nearly white, that she was mistaken for a white woman. She was, in all probability, her master's daughter or sister." This liberation of a runaway slave was no isolated incident for the Illinois 9th. When this unit raided Florence, Mississippi, on May 31, 1863, it freed more than two hundred enslaved people.

German-born Emil Guelich also served in the 9th Illinois. An abolitionist who participated in southwestern Illinois's Underground Railroad before enlisting, Guelich served as chief surgeon. When his regiment was in battle and he was not needed to treat the wounded, however, Guelich would seize his revolver and join the other men in combat. Guelich could be a healer or killer, depending on the situation.

Following the Civil War, any number of Union veterans claimed to be the "Drummer Boy of Shiloh," who was celebrated in a popular song composed in 1862 following that bloody battle. Some area residents believe that Greene County teenager Edward L. Hager deserves that recognition. Hager briefly served in the fife and drum corps of the 61st Illinois Infantry, which saw action at Shiloh, where he displayed extraordinary courage under fire.

These men voluntarily enlisted in the Union army and played an integral role in saving the Union and destroying slavery. Our nation owes them much, and it is time—indeed past time—that their stories were told.

UNION COLLEGES

SHURTLEFF COLLEGE

One of the most influential figures in American Christianity, John Mason Peck, was born near Litchfield, Connecticut, on October 31, 1789, and converted at a revival in 1807. Peck embraced the Baptist denomination and began preaching in 1811. He served two Baptist congregations in New York and, despite his lack of formal education, started teaching to supplement his income. Peck was formally ordained as a Baptist minister in 1813.

This energetic convert with a passion to spread the gospel was sent as a missionary to the Missouri Territory in 1817, which he reached after an arduous four-month journey in a one-horse wagon with his wife and four children. Just one month after arriving in St. Louis, he opened the Western Mission Academy in St. Louis. The academy was historically important as the earliest attempt by the Baptists to establish a school in the West, but it was not successful. A bawdy river town at that time, the Gateway City proved to be a less than ideal site for the Christian boarding school than Peck had in mind. He began to scout the area for a new location, a journey that took him to the Illinois village of Upper Alton in southwestern Illinois. Peck later wrote that early Upper Alton consisted of forty to fifty families living in log cabins, shanties, covered wagons and camps. Twenty-five or thirty boys and girls attended a rudimentary school taught by a man whom Peck deemed "a backwoods fellow." The ambitious Peck decided that a boarding school in such a primitive settlement simply would not work. The school was relocated to St. Charles, Missouri.

Peck moved in 1822 to a farm at the Rock Spring settlement, which was located near present-day Fairview Heights in St. Clair County. Edward Coles was elected governor of Illinois that year as an antislavery candidate in a four-way race. The state legislature, which was dominated by proslavery elements, responded by calling for a referendum that would authorize a convention to amend the constitution and make Illinois a slave state. The pro- and antislavery forces in the Prairie State engaged in a prolonged battle. Politicians made impassioned speeches, newspapers waged wars of words and Illinoisans who felt strongly about this critical issue frequently engaged in public brawls. Peck steadfastly opposed slavery and assumed a prominent

Baptist missionary John Mason Peck founded Shurtleff College, which became a Union bastion during the Civil War. *Public domain image.*

role in fighting the referendum. When the measure was finally put to a statewide vote in 1824, it was soundly defeated. The epic referendum is discussed at length in *Abolitionism and the Civil War in Southwestern Illinois* (The History Press, 2011).

This missionary and educator successfully engaged in a number of endeavors during his lifetime. He founded the *Pioneer* in 1829, which was the first Baptist periodical in the West. A few years later, he began publishing the *Illinois Sunday-School Banner*. But Peck's vision of founding a Christian boarding school in the West remained unwavering. He realized that much of the success of the Baptist denomination depended on having ministers with the kind of solid education they could obtain only in a seminary staffed with good teachers. A board of trustees was elected on January 1, 1827, and the Rock Spring Seminary formally came into existence.

The seminary was housed in a two-story frame building that had one-story wings on either side. Women students roomed in another building. Reverend J.T. Bradley, an accomplished preacher and strict disciplinarian, served as the first principal, with Peck assuming this position the following year. John Messenger, a surveyor for the federal government who had worked with Peck and Coles to defeat the proslavery referendum, taught mathematics and Latin. Ebenezer Marsh, who later became a prominent druggist and banker in Alton, also served on the faculty. His son, also named Ebenezer Marsh, taught at Shurtleff College from 1854 to 1875.

Peck and the board of trustees longed for a better location for the school. At a meeting held in Edwardsville on July 26, 1832, the board decided that the seminary should be moved to Upper Alton. The ramshackle hodgepodge of shanties and covered wagons of a decade earlier had given rise to a thriving community that would welcome an institution of higher learning. Upper Alton's location near three great rivers—the Mississippi, Missouri and Illinois—made it accessible by steamboat, so it could draw students from the western and southern states.

Hubbel Loomis, the newly elected principal, journeyed east to secure funding for the seminary. A native of Vermont, Loomis was an abolitionist who, in 1837, along with fellow southwestern Illinois abolitionists Elijah Lovejoy, Charles Hunter and Thaddeus Hurlbut, co-founded the Illinois Anti-Slavery Society in Upper Alton. The school, now called Alton Seminary, was soon ready to accept students. Academic Hall, the school's first building, was a two-story brick structure. The ground floor contained the chapel and library, while the second floor held two rows of dormitories.

The school took well to its new location. Alton College of Illinois, as the seminary became known, was granted a charter by the Illinois legislature in 1835. Later that year, Dr. Benjamin Shurtleff of Boston, a Harvard-educated physician, donated $10,000 to the college with three provisions: half the sum must be used for building purposes, the other half was to be used to establish a professorship of rhetoric and elocution and, finally, the school must be renamed Shurtleff College. On January 12, 1836, the board of trustees formally changed the name of the school.

Peck died at his Rock Spring residence in 1858. Vitally interested in Shurtleff College to the very end, he left a number of his books to its library. Peck's opposition to the proposed constitutional convention that would have made Illinois a slave state and Loomis's role in co-founding the Illinois Anti-Slavery Society, as well as serving as one of the society's vice-presidents, firmly placed Shurtleff College in the antislavery column. During the antebellum period, the school was an important station on the Underground Railroad.

When the Civil War began, Shurtleff College rallied to the Union cause. Austen K. de Blois, a Shurtleff College president who later wrote a history of the school, observed, "Throughout the entire progress of the war, the faculty and students seem to have been a unit in their support of the Northern armies, though the Southland was so near." He also stated that nearly two hundred Shurtleff students and graduates "took up arms in defense of the Union." Enrollment plummeted as young scholars abandoned their studies to enlist in the Union army. The entire graduating class of 1864, as well as a large number of that year's undergraduates, joined the army. While the precise number of Shurtleff casualties is unknown, De Blois noted that six members of the class of 1867 left school before the completion of their freshmen year to enlist. Three of the six—Charles Ives, Harlow Street and David Wear—were killed.

Shurtleff College alumnus Franklin Moore distinguished himself during the Civil War. Born on September 2, 1826, he was the tenth—and last—child of Abel and Mary Moore, the pioneer couple who lost two earlier children during the Wood River Massacre in 1814. That tragedy is covered in *Murder and Mayhem in Southwestern Illinois* (The History Press, 2021). Franklin attended a school taught by Sophia Loomis, the daughter of Hubbel Loomis, that was held in his parents' log cabin. He later enrolled at Shurtleff College.

Franklin Moore formed an independent cavalry unit that was mustered into the Union army as Company D of the 2nd Illinois Cavalry. *From* History of Madison County, Illinois.

Readers of *Abolitionism and the Civil War in Southwestern Illinois* will recall the role Franklin Moore played in keeping Union arms out of Rebel hands while still a civilian. Moore could have rested on his laurels during the Civil War. His devotion to the Union, however, compelled him to enter the conflict. Although heavily in debt, Moore left his livelihood to raise an independent cavalry unit in Upper Alton on July 4, 1861, that he named the Madison County Rangers in honor of his father's service with the Territorial Rangers during the War of 1812. Its members assumed responsibility for providing their own horses, weapons and other equipment.

Moore formally enlisted on July 20 in Upper Alton. He led his men to Camp Butler, which was located east of Springfield, where the Madison County Rangers were mustered into the Union army on August 12 as Company D of the 2nd Illinois Cavalry. An 1882 Madison County history states that Company D had "no abiding place but operated from the northern border of the Confederacy to the Gulf. It first saw action in the Cape Girardeau [Missouri] area, where it battled Rebel forces under the command of Jeff Thompson."

James Webster, a Confederate bushwhacker, drew a bead on Moore during a skirmish in Tennessee, but his musket misfired. Moore then charged the bushwhacker, who fully expected to be cut down by the Yankee's sword. Instead, Moore took the young Rebel as a prisoner. Webster later took an oath of allegiance to the Union and was released from custody. In a strange twist of fate, Webster eventually moved to Alton and became an employee of the city. He completed the repudiation of his Confederate past by becoming a staunch Republican.

At least eleven members of Company D died during the war, three of whom were killed in action. These three privates—Christian Commell, Albert Jordan and Alonzo McCurdy—fell at Coldwater, Mississippi, in 1863. Corporal Andrew J. Dale went missing in action on February 23, 1864. Moore was wounded by a rifle ball on August 27, 1862, but returned to active service just a week later. He was promoted to major on July 11, 1864. When Company D's term of service expired in the summer of 1864, it was reorganized and continued in active service until the end of the war. The record shows that Moore's men killed more than 100 Confederates and took more than 1,200 prisoners. They also captured about 1,000 horses and mules, as well as enemy munitions and other equipment. The Madison County history concluded that "[n]one in the service experienced greater hardships or made a better record than Company D." Regarding Moore, this history noted, "Such were the services he rendered his country on the battle-field, that he received the sobriquet of 'Fighting Frank.'" Moore and his Madison County Rangers were mustered out on November 11, 1865.

After the war, Moore returned to farming in Wood River township. In 1876, four years after the death of his wife, he purchased for his home the Old Rock House in Upper Alton, one of the most historic buildings in southern Illinois. Owned by abolitionist Thaddeus Hurlbut in 1837, the Old Rock House that year hosted the founding convention of the Illinois Anti-

RESIDENCE OF MAJOR FRANK MOORE, UPPER ALTON, ILL.

Tom, Franklin Moore's Civil War horse, is depicted in this sketch of Moore's Upper Alton home. *From* History of Madison County, Illinois.

Slavery Society. It also served as an Underground Railroad station. Like many Union veterans, Moore became a Republican Party stalwart. The impoverished farmer of years past became a man of means who owned a portion of the family farm on Rattan's Prairie, a farm on Woodburn Road and no small amount of real estate in Upper Alton.

Thirteen years after the war's end, Moore's old Company D suffered a belated casualty. The June 27, 1878 edition of the *Alton Evening Telegraph* carried this brief notice:

Major Frank Moore's famous war horse which carried its gallant rider through five years of campaigning from the beginning to the close of the Civil War died last Friday, aged 21 years. The horse was wounded seven times while in service. Faithful Old Tom was buried on Sunday morning at ten o'clock in the bottom near Shield's Branch, just west of Upper Alton. The funeral cortege consisted of about forty people. A few volleys were fired over his grave.

Moore enjoyed reminiscing about his service but was troubled by the possibility that Company D might have been deprived of a triumph that would have secured its place in history. The August 3, 1888 edition of the *Alton Evening Telegraph* carried an article that noted:

Maj. Frank Moore says that after the surrender of Lee's army to Grant, in April, 1865, he was in command of the 2nd Illinois Cavalry in pursuit of Jeff Davis. Near Eufaula, Georgia, his regiment belonging to Gen. Grierson's brigade was ordered back. Had this not been the case the major has no doubt but that his force would have captured the arch traitor within two days, for soon after the retrograde movement commenced Wilson's cavalry was met, a detachment of which, following the same route Maj. Moore had intended taking, apprehended the fugitive chief of the Southern Confederacy.

The reporter must have misquoted Moore. Eufaula is located in Alabama, not Georgia. A detachment of Wilson's cavalry apprehended Davis on May 10 near Irwinville, Georgia.

The old warrior remained in touch with his men through annual reunions. The *Telegraph* in 1881 noted that Moore and fifty-four of his cavalrymen met at Bloomington, Illinois, for a reunion of veterans that featured an appearance by Ulysses S. Grant. He also held "campfires," a term used by Union Civil War veterans for reunions, each year on his birthday and invited Civil War veterans to attend and share their memories of the conflict. For the 1904 campfire, Moore extended invitations to Colonel J.Q. Morrison, commander of the 14th Mississippi Infantry during the Civil War, and Colonel Vance Cobb of Mississippi. The *Telegraph* noted that "Major Moore and Col. Morrison's command had often fought each other on the battlefield, and as they know the personal bravery of each other, they are especial friends and have been so since the close of the war, even before it was closed." Morrison and Cobb had journeyed north that year to visit the St. Louis World's Fair, which gave them the opportunity to attend Moore's campfire.

Unfortunately, this was Moore's last campfire. He died on July 12, 1905, at the Old Rock House. Since his home wasn't large enough to accommodate the hundreds of mourners who wished to pay their final respects, Moore's coffin was placed in the same yard where the campfires had been held for so many years. Moore was buried at Oakwood Cemetery (now known as Upper Alton Cemetery), where representatives of the Grand Army of the Republic, an organization composed of Union veterans, conducted a graveside service. A number of Company D veterans were in attendance, some of whom served as honorary pallbearers.

Moore had always taken pride in the care of his property and evidently wanted to make certain that his eternal resting place was properly maintained as well. His will stipulated that his son, Frank, a Chicago newspaperman, erect over his grave a monument that must not cost less than $500, which is about $12,000 in today's money. Frank was also required by the terms of the will to visit his father's grave at least twice a year to make certain the monument was in good condition.

In addition to Franklin Moore, readers of *Abolitionism and the Civil War in Southwestern Illinois* will also recall Wilberforce Lovejoy Hurlbut. The youngest child and only son of Thaddeus and Abigail Hurlbut, Wilberforce Lovejoy Hurlbut was named in honor of two famous abolitionists: the British abolitionist William Wilberforce and Elijah Lovejoy, who had been his father's dear friend and fellow ally in the Illinois abolitionist movement. Wilberforce Lovejoy Hurlbut enrolled in Shurtleff College, which was located just a short distance from his home. A brilliant student, he excelled in Greek and mathematics. Against his parents' wishes, he left college in the middle of his senior year in 1862 to enlist in the Union army. For Hurlbut, the Civil War wasn't about merely saving the Union. It was a noble crusade to rid the United States of slavery, and he wanted to be part of it.

The Upper Alton home of Wilberforce Lovejoy Hurlbut, who dropped out of Shurtleff College to join the Union army and went missing in action during the Battle of the Wilderness. *From the* Telegraph *(Alton, IL).*

Hurlbut distinguished himself in combat. He fought at Antietam, led the 5th Michigan Regiment at Chancellorsville and was wounded at Gettysburg. He went missing in action on May 6, 1864, during the Battle of the Wilderness. It was soon determined that he had been shot to death during that engagement. His body was never recovered.

A truly heartrending letter came to my attention since I wrote of Hurlbut in *Abolitionism and the Civil War*. It was written by Abigail Hurlbut and sent to Clara Barton. Hurlbut was desperate to learn more information regarding her late son. Barton, who had tended wounded soldiers in hospitals and even on battlefields during the war, had been appointed by Lincoln in March 1865 to the position of General Correspondent for the Friends of Paroled Prisoners. According to her biography on the American Battlefield trust website:

> *Her job was to respond to anxious inquiries from the friends and relatives of missing soldiers by locating them among the prison rolls, parole rolls, or casualty lists at the camps in Annapolis, Maryland. To assist in this enormous task, Barton established the Bureau of Records of Missing Men of the Armies of the United States and published Rolls of Missing Men to be posted across the country. It was at her insistence that the anonymous graves at Andersonville prison were identified and marked.*

Abigail Hurlbut's letter to Barton is contained in the archives of the Clara Barton Missing Soldiers Office Museum. It reads:

Upper Alton, Illinois Sept. 26th 1865
Miss Barton Dear Madam,

I approach you with my great sorrow, but hardly indulge the hope that you can do anything for me. My darling boy, my only son, was reported killed in the Battle of the Wilderness, May 6th, 1864. His body was not found, and the hope was entertained by his Regiment and clutched at by myself, that wounded he had fallen into the hands of the Enemy, a prisoner and not dead.

After various fruitless efforts to obtain information, [Confederate] *General* [James] *Longstreet courteously ordered an examination in the southern prisons, and we obtained a certificate from each that no such name had ever been received. After all our investigations we are led to the conclusion that he died on the battle field, or mortally wounded, was conveyed to some farm house and may have there been buried. He was Captain of company D, Fifth Michigan Infantry. His sword, a cavalry sabre, had his name engraved upon it. Wilber Hurlbut, Fifth Michigan Infantry.*

He was in Hancock's Corps, Birney's Division, Hay's Brigade. He had command of the Regiment at the time he fell. Had charged the enemy through a wood and was in the vicinity of Spottsylvania. Our men were heavily pressed and fell back. Captain Hurlbut was missing. A man, by the name of Luke Stanton, told an officer that he saw him fall. We have been unable to find Luke Stanton & have never ascertained to what Regiment he belonged, but learned he was soon after mustered out of the service. Captain Miller, Aid to [Union] *General* [Winfield Scott] *Hancock, made such efforts as he could, and other of his comrades did all in their power to learn his fate but we elicit nothing. If he died on the battlefield, I would that I knew it and if he died at a farm house, how much I wish to know it.*

For his sword I would give a handsome reward. Anything that was his would be most precious to me and nothing to strangers. Some articles of toilet he had with him have his name. Whatever of money found on his person was of course the spoil of war. My son was twenty-two years old. Wore no moustache or beard. Was about six feet in height. When in College he was rather spare, but the outdoor life of the army had given him a robust appearance. He entered the army as Aid to General [Israel B.] *Richardson. After that officer's lamented death, he served in the Michigan*

Fifth. He had participated in more than twenty battles. Was severely wounded at Gettysburg, but from which he wholly recovered.

The enemy held the battle ground of the Wilderness and should anything ever be revealed in regard to my dear boy, it would probably come from some Rebel source, unless indeed some of our men captured at the time should know something. [Confederate] *General* [Richard S.] *Ewell held the field there for sometime. It may be well to add my son's name to the many missing ones, and could you by any means give to me any knowledge of the last resting place of my darling one you would confer such a favor as none less desolate than myself can appreciate.*

May God bless you in your humane efforts and abundantly reward you.

Mrs. T.B. Hurlbut, Upper Alton, Illinois.
P.S. I neglected to mention that my son had dark hazel eyes. Hair almost black.

Jake Wynn, director of interpretation at the Clara Barton Missing Soldiers Office Museum, added this comment following Hurlbut's letter on the museum's website: "Wilbur T. [*sic*] Hurlbut's body was never identified. It was likely moved to Fredericksburg National Cemetery with thousands of other unknown Union dead in the years after the Civil War."

There is also the possibility that his corpse could have been incinerated by one of the fires that raged in the Wilderness during the battle. In any event, Wilberforce Lovejoy Hurlbut's name is inscribed on the Hurlbut family monument at Alton Cemetery, which is also the final resting place of Elijah Lovejoy. The inscription notes his 1841 birth and the fact that he went missing on May 6, 1864, after the Battle of the Wilderness.

Hurlbut's sword was never returned to his family. It was probably taken by a Confederate soldier as he lay dead on the battlefield. Well-made swords were especially prized by the Rebels. Perhaps in some southern attic a cavalry saber that bears the inscription "Wilber Hurlbut, Fifth Michigan Infantry" lies forgotten.

At least three Union generals studied at Shurtleff. In the nineteenth century, the college included a preparatory department that, according to De Blois, was "open to students of any age and acquirements" and "intended to fit boys for college or prepare them directly for the business of life." Nathaniel Pope, who lived in the old French-founded town of Kaskaskia, Illinois, and served as a federal judge in early Illinois, sent his children to Shurtleff College because it would afford them the kind of education that was ordinarily denied to young people living on the frontier. Shurtleff's preparatory department gave young John Pope the education he needed to enter the United States Military Academy at West Point, from which he graduated in 1842.

Pope served under Zachary Taylor in the war with Mexico and engaged in survey work for the army during the pre–Civil War years. He was one of four army officers who were selected to escort Lincoln to Washington, D.C., in 1861 to assume the presidency. In May 1861, Pope was appointed to the rank of brigadier general and ordered to recruit Illinois volunteers for the Union army. A number of these recruits were Shurtleff College men.

Serving in the Western Department under Major General John Frémont, whom he intensely disliked and lobbied to have removed from command, Pope defeated Confederate general Sterling Price at Blackwater, Missouri. Frémont's replacement, Major General Henry Halleck, gave Pope command of the Army of the Mississippi in February 1862 and ordered him to secure the Mississippi River for the Union. Pope seized Rebel stronghold New Madrid, Missouri, and laid plans to capture the Confederate fort on Island No. 10, which was so named because it was the tenth island in the Mississippi below its juncture with the Ohio River. Confederate batteries on the Tennessee shore also helped to make this S-shaped stretch of the Mississippi impassable for Union river traffic. To seize this fort, Pope made use of armored gunboats, a new type of naval vessel designed by engineer Samuel Pook and built by James B. Eads at shipyards in Carondolet, a small town near St. Louis, and Mound City, located in deep southern Illinois.

Eads, an engineering genius who had established his reputation by constructing a diving bell that allowed him to salvage steamboat wreckage from the bottom of the Mississippi, was awarded a federal contract in August 1861 to build seven ironclad gunboats. Each ironclad was 175 feet long, with wooden sides covered by 2.5 inches of iron plates. Five long steam boilers powered the single paddlewheel. The iron plates allowed these boats to withstand enemy assault, while the

General John Pope captured Island No. 10 in the Mississippi River but was badly defeated at the Second Battle of Bull Run. *Library of Congress.*

thirteen heavy cannons on each craft ensured their capacity to inflict lethal bombardment on enemy fortifications.

Pope ordered his engineers to cut a river channel that would allow the vessels transporting federal forces to bypass the fort and its cannons. Soon after daylight on April 7, the ironclad *Carondolet* steamed past Island No. 10, followed by the *Pittsburgh*. According to Maurice Melton in his article "The Struggle for Rebel Island No. 10, Smoke Across the Water," the Rebel battery "fought for an hour under intense cannonading, then its gun crews fled to the woods," with the other battery crews soon following suit.

With the shore cleared of Confederate batteries, Pope launched his attack on the island. Overwhelmed by such superior force, the fort surrendered. The conquest of Island No.10 was a stunning victory for Pope and the Union. The North now controlled the Mississippi as far south as Memphis.

Pope's victories in the west brought him a promotion to major general and assignment to command the Army of Virginia. However, he was routed at the Second Battle of Bull Run in August 1863 by three of the South's greatest generals: Stonewall Jackson, James Longstreet and Robert E. Lee. He was removed from command and reassigned to Minnesota, where he spent the remainder of the Civil War battling the Sioux. Pope served as governor of the Reconstruction Third Military District in the postwar South until he was removed by President Andrew Johnson. He spent the remainder of his military career fighting Apache Indians in the West. John Pope died in 1892.

John Cook, born in Belleville in 1825, also studied at Shurtleff. Ninian Edwards, his maternal grandfather, served the Prairie State as its governor and U.S. senator. Cook's father, Daniel Cook, was a member of Congress. John Cook carried on this tradition of public service by winning the office of mayor of Springfield, Illinois, in 1855.

Cook in 1858 formed the Springfield Zouave Grays, an independent militia, and served as its captain. The Grays became the nucleus of Company I of the 7th Illinois Volunteer Regiment, which was mustered in on April 25, 1861—the first Illinois regiment of the Civil War. Cook served as its colonel. He distinguished himself during the campaign to capture Fort Donelson in Tennessee in1862, when his troops took out a key Confederate battery. Without artillery support, the Confederate line collapsed in Cook's sector of the battle. In recognition of his contribution to the Union victory, Cook was promoted to brigadier general of volunteers.

Like Pope, Cook also spent time battling the Sioux. Unlike Pope, however, Cook returned to Civil War duty when he was assigned to command the military district of Illinois in 1864. By the time the conflict ended, Cook had attained the rank of brevet major general. He returned to politics and served in the Illinois General Assembly. He died in 1910.

John M. Palmer—unquestionably the most historically significant graduate of Shurtleff College—was born in Kentucky in 1817. His family in 1831 moved to Paddock's Prairie, a pioneer Madison County settlement located midway between Upper Alton and Edwardsville. Motorists who drive Illinois Route 140 cross Paddock Creek, the only tangible reminder of this little settlement's existence. As a young man, Palmer enrolled in Shurtleff College. The board of trustees allowed the impoverished young scholar to work his way through school and even gave him the sum of twenty dollars to set up a cooper's shop on the college campus. Palmer's success upon graduating from Shurtleff proved that the board had indeed invested its money wisely.

He became a lawyer and won election as a judge in Macoupin County. Palmer learned the region's hostility toward abolitionists—or even those thought to be abolitionists—when he presided over a case and admitted the affidavit of a Black man as testimony, which so enraged his fellow citizens that a mob was organized to lynch him as an abolitionist and would doubtless have carried their threats into execution but for his well-known courage, great size and physical strength.

According to historian William Henry Milburn, Palmer "had been by all odds the most popular citizen and officer of the county" and previously had been heavily favored to win reelection to the bench. Instead, he was overwhelmingly defeated—simply because he had been labeled an abolitionist.

Palmer entered politics as a Democrat, but his opposition to slavery led him to co-found the Republican Party in Illinois. He became friends with Lincoln and played a leading role in securing the 1860 Republican presidential nomination for his fellow Illinoisan. When the Civil War broke out, Palmer entered the Union army as a colonel and rose to the rank of major general. He and his troops fought at Battle of Stones River and the Battle of Chickamauga and in the Chattanooga Campaign. Palmer also participated in Sherman's March to the Sea.

Lincoln appointed Palmer commander of the Department of Kentucky, a position he formally assumed on February 18, 1865. In his posthumously published autobiography, Palmer observed that Congress on March 10, 1865, passed a law declaring that "the wives and children of colored men who have heretofore enlisted, or who may hereafter enlist in the military service of the United States, are free." Palmer announced this landmark legislation on

Shurtleff College graduate John M. Palmer rose to the rank of major general during the Civil War. *Library of Congress, Illinois State Library Heritage Project.*

March 12, when he released Order No. 10 "to the colored people of the department."

It should be noted, however, that the slaves of Kentucky played a significant role in their own liberation. The policies initiated by Palmer and General S.G. Burbridge, his predecessor in Kentucky, would have proved futile had that state's enslaved population "not taken the initiative by passively refusing to act the part of slaves any longer," as Lowell H. Harrison argued in his article "Slavery in Kentucky: A Civil War Casualty." Contact with the Union army "had taught the slaves much about the wage system," and "blacks abandoned slavery in Kentucky in increased numbers." Still, these self-liberated people weren't legally free.

"The negroes in Kentucky believed that I had unlimited power, and one of those impalpable rumors reached the negro population that if they would come to Louisville on the Fourth of July [1865], I would declare them to be free." Palmer insisted that he had never made such a promise to the Black population of Kentucky. Nonetheless, He recalled that "negroes from all the surrounding counties were moving on to Louisville with the expectation that I would give them freedom." The old general wrote:

> *The advance of the negroes began to arrive on July 3d, and a committee of them waited on me at my headquarters to know "at what hour and at what place would I declare their freedom." I told the committee that "I had no authority to set them free," and tried to persuade them to go home quietly and wait, and they would be free after awhile, anyhow. There was a circus at the time in Louisville, performing under the direction of a man named Noyes, with whom I had formed quite an acquaintance from frequent attendance upon his performances, and through Colonel Mark Mundy, Noyes had offered me his gilded chariot and the piebald horses to take myself and company to the fair grounds to hear Parsons, who had been an actor, and was now a Methodist preacher, read the "Declaration of Independence." The next morning, I took the chariot and the piebald horses, with Parsons, Colonel Mundy and General Brisbane for company, and reached the fair grounds about ten o'clock on the Fourth of July.*

Messengers from Louisville informed Palmer that "the city was full of negroes who were waiting for me to set them free." He drove the chariot back to Louisville, only to learn that nearly all of the community's Black population "had assembled in a grove south of the city" to await Palmer's arrival:

> *When I reached the mass of colored people I was lifted over their heads and placed upon a platform....When the tumult had partially subsided, I said, "My countrymen, you are substantially free!" They never heard the word "substantially." There went up a shout which could have been heard for a mile.*

While the crowd rejoiced, Palmer wondered how President Andrew Johnson and Secretary of War Edwin Stanton would react upon hearing news of his proclamation. Nonetheless, he resolved "to 'drive the last nail in the coffin' of the 'institution' even if it cost me the command of the department." When the shouting had died down a bit, Palmer again addressed the crowd. "My countrymen, you are free, and while I command in this department the military forces of the United States will defend your right to freedom." Hearing themselves addressed as "countrymen" by a white man must have been a tremendously powerful experience for the audience. It implied equality rather than subservience.

"Slavery practically ended in Kentucky on July 4, 1865," Palmer wrote. He reported his action to Johnson and Stanton, "and as a consequence on the 25th of July the following order was issued" by the Adjutant General's Office of the War Department. General Order 129 reads:

> *To secure equal justice and the same personal liberty to the freedmen as to other citizens and inhabitants, all orders issued by post, district and other commanders, adopting any system of passes for them, or subjecting them to any restraints or punishments not imposed on other classes are declared void.*
>
> *Neither white nor black will be restrained from seeking employment elsewhere when they cannot obtain it at a just compensation at their homes and when not bound by voluntary agreement, nor will they be hindered from traveling from place to place on proper and legitimate business.*

Palmer was correct when he told that Independence Day Black audience that they were "substantially" free. The Kentucky legislature on February 24, 1865, had rejected the Thirteenth Amendment, which is why Black

Kentuckians looked to Palmer to declare them free. Slavery legally ended in Kentucky when the necessary three-quarters of our states ratified the Thirteenth Amendment and it went into effect on December 6, 1865. The State of Kentucky belatedly ratified the Thirteenth Amendment in 1976, when the United States celebrated its bicentennial.

In addition to symbolically ending slavery in Kentucky, Palmer also earned acclaimed for battling the Confederate guerrillas who pillaged and murdered Unionists. As he explained in his memoirs:

> *General Burbridge, who had preceded me in command of the district of Kentucky…had attempted to terrify the guerrillas by hanging their friends. He was in the habit of selecting four, by lot from his military prison, and having taken them near to the spot of the outrage, hang them. I chose to pursue a different course, and made war upon the guerrillas personally. For example, the guerrilla Marion having sent me notice that he had captured Dr. Montgomery Miller, assistant surgeon of one of the Indiana regiments, and would hang him unless Medkiff or Magruder, who were both in the military prison, should be discharged. I issued an order dated April 11, 1865 that "neither Medkiff nor Magruder will be discharged, but will be tried, and if found guilty of acts contrary to the rules of civilized warfare, will be punished accordingly; and upon reliable information that Dr. Miller has been injured, both will be executed at once. The above notice is given at the request of Marion that an answer be returned through the newspapers."*

Palmer returned to politics after the war, although his political allegiance often shifted. He was elected governor of Illinois as a Republican and a U.S. senator as a Democrat and ran for president in 1896 as the candidate of the National Democrats, which was a faction of the Democratic Party that supported the gold standard. Ironically, Palmer's running mate was Simon Bolivar Buckner, the former governor of Kentucky who had served as a lieutenant general in the Confederate army. John M. Palmer died in 1900 at age eighty-three.

Shurtleff College continued to prosper through the late nineteenth and early twentieth centuries. Andrew Carnegie, the wealthy industrialist and philanthropist, pledged to give the college a $15,000 library building if Shurtleff secured an equal amount for maintenance. The necessary funds were acquired, and construction began in 1911. The new library was formally dedicated at the 1912 commencement.

Most of Shurtleff's students were drawn from southwestern Illinois, and the majority of its graduates remained in the area. The 1946 edition of the Alton High School *Tattler* listed twelve faculty members who were Shurtleff College alumni.

Shurtleff College in 1950 had seven hundred students, the highest enrollment in its history. That year's graduating class numbered ninety-nine, another all-time high for the college. The class of 1950 erected a memorial on campus that stands to this day—the lettering SHURTLEFF COLLEGE, atop a globe, telescope and desk, with an old-fashioned quill pen, all cast in wrought iron over a gateway.

Shurtleff's president, Dr. Roland E. Turnbull, in his preface to the 1956 edition of *The Retrospect*, the annual yearbook, wrote that in an ever-changing world, Shurtleff College reaffirmed its commitment to Jesus Christ and the importance of Christian education. His words rang of optimism for Shurtleff College's future. On June 30, 1957, however, financial hardship forced this Illinois institution to cease operation, although its last twenty-eight students graduated in 1958. It had been the oldest Baptist school west of the Appalachian Mountains.

The Shurtleff College campus was acquired by Southern Illinois University, which began holding classes at the site in 1958. Southwestern Illinois residents were still afforded the opportunity to secure a college education in their own community. The old Shurtleff campus became the Southern Illinois University School of Dental Medicine in 1972. A classroom building at the Edwardsville campus of Southern Illinois University is named after John Mason Peck. The library at the Edwardsville campus is named after the martyred abolitionist Elijah Lovejoy.

Vestiges of Shurtleff College remain on the old campus. Besides the class of 1950 memorial, three other classes left tangible reminders of their years at Shurtleff: a concrete tête-à-tête inscribed with the words CARPE DIEM, courtesy of the class of 1909; a sundial erected by Shurtleff's class of 1927 in honor of the college's centennial; and a stone bench from the class of 1948 that rests outside Loomis Hall. A wishing well, inscribed ALUMNI WELL but carrying no date, was sealed shut decades ago. Motorists making their way through Upper Alton are reminded of Shurtleff College simply by the names on the street signs. The old campus is located at the corner of Seminary Street (Alton Seminary, the school's name after relocating to Alton) and College Avenue (Shurtleff College).

McKendree College

Named in honor of William McKendree, who was the first American-born bishop of the Methodist Church, McKendree College was founded in 1828 by that denomination. The Methodists built their college on eight acres in the St. Clair County village of Lebanon that were purchased for three dollars per acre. Just one year earlier, Risdon M. Moore had been born near the old French village of Cahokia, which is now known as Cahokia Heights. Moore enrolled in McKendree in 1845 and graduated five years later. He then served as a tutor in Latin and Greek at his alma mater. Four years later, he became the college's professor of mathematics and astronomy.

Much like Shurtleff College, McKendree College rallied to the Union cause when the war broke out. At the beginning of the conflict, the combined faculty and students of the school numbered fewer than two hundred men. "It seems likely," according to a McKendree College history, "that altogether there were not less than a hundred and fifty who were in the army and students at McKendree either before or after their war service." Since a few new students enrolled in the college each year, the college "was kept going in spite of the large number who entered the army."

At least two prominent Union generals attended McKendree before enrolling at West Point: James H. Wilson and Wesley Merritt. As mentioned earlier, cavalry under Wilson's command captured Jefferson Davis in 1865. Years after the Civil War, Merritt became superintendent of the U.S. Military Academy. Nonetheless, it was Risdon Moore who forged McKendree's reputation as a Union bastion and secured its honored place in Civil War history.

A Republican who was acquainted with Lincoln, Moore was described by a former student as a scholar with no passion for war but whose love for the Union compelled him to take up arms. Moore was commissioned a colonel and ordered to command the 117th Illinois Infantry, which was organized in September 1862. This unit became known as the "McKendree Regiment" because of the large number of men from that college who served in it. Samuel H. Deneen, another McKendree faculty member, became the regiment's adjunct. Lieutenant Colonel Jonathan Merriam, who had attended McKendree for one year in the 1850s before ill health forced him to drop out, was second in command.

The men of the 117th Illinois Infantry completed their basic training at Camp Butler and were then transported by steamboat down the Mississippi to Fort Pickering at Memphis. Moore wrote a brief history of the 117th for

Risdon Moore commanded the 117th Illinois Infantry, which was known as the "McKendree Brigade." *Missouri History Museum.*

the 1905 edition of the *McKendree Pigskin*, a college publication. He recalled that the men were issued .69-caliber Belgian-made muskets that "after bursting a cap eight or ten times they would no longer explode one…no one could tell us what was the matter with our guns, and they were all alike." These Belgian weapons were finally examined by none other than General William Tecumseh Sherman, who concluded that "the defect was irreparable."

Since soldiers without reliable muskets could hardly be sent into combat, the 117th was "kept to man that fort with its hundred and twenty heavy guns for nearly two years." The men were occasionally sent out on scout duty and battled small Rebel forces in Tennessee and Arkansas but saw no major action until the summer of 1863, when they were dispatched to Helena, Arkansas. The 117th joined with Union general Benjamin M. Prentiss to defeat the combined forces of Confederate generals Sterling Price and John S. Marmaduke, who, according to Moore, fled "into the Arkansas woods to rest."

On January 25, 1864, the 117th was assigned to the Army of the Tennessee, 16th Army Corps, 3rd Division, 3rd Brigade, under the command of Brigadier General Andrew J. Smith. Moore and his men fought "almost daily until we entered Meridian [Mississippi], February 14, under the boom of cannon and the rattle of rifles, the 117th in the lead." Upon entering Meridian, "we worked for eight days destroying railroads, with corn for rations for man and beast."

Moore's memoir is harshly critical of Union major general Nathaniel Banks's disastrous Red River Campaign, which targeted Shreveport, Louisiana, for capture, as well as a huge quantity of Confederate cotton. Moore bitterly observed:

> *Banks, to display his army and his lack of generalship, had placed our command a day's march behind his rear, and besides this had cumbered us with his baggage and a part of his supply train. Hence we were fully twenty miles from the battlefield on the eighth [of April 1864], but hearing the boom of cannon on the afternoon of the eighth, we abandoned*

all trains and hastened to the front at a quick step and met our routed forces at Pleasant Hill at dusk. Their condition gave an idea of our stampede at Bull Run. We fought the battle almost alone on the ninth and won a great victory, driving the rebels from seven to twenty-one miles.

The Tupelo Campaign brought the McKendree Brigade into conflict with Confederate general Nathan Bedford Forrest, whose cavalry posed a threat to Sherman's supply line. On July 14, the 117th played a key role in repulsing a Confederate attack. Moore attested that his men "bore the most conspicuous part and I accord to this regiment all credit for the prompt manner in which they met and repulsed the enemy."

The 117th was dispatched to Nashville in December to aid Union major general George Thomas, who was battling the forces of Confederate general John Bell Hood. During the charge on Shy's Hill, the 117th exposed itself to deadly battery fire and captured one hundred prisoners, as well as two cannons. Private Wilbur F. Moore of the 117th, who was not related to Risdon Moore, captured the flag and flag-bearer of this Rebel battery. According to Lieutenant Colonel Jonathan Merriam, Moore was "far in advance of the line when he did so." For such heroism, Wilbur F. Moore received the Medal of Honor.

The McKendree Brigade saw its final action during the Siege of Mobile, the last major stronghold of the Confederacy. This Alabama city had been protected by Spanish Fort and Fort Blakely, which quickly fell to Union forces on April 8–9, 1865, since most of their Confederate defenders had been evacuated. Moore recalled finding a letter written by the colonel of an Alabama regiment. The unfolded missive was addressed to his mother and read, "Dear Mother: You have or will hear of the capture of Spanish Fort by the Yankees, but I write to assure you that there are not enough Yankees in Alabama to capture us in a month."

Moore proudly reported, "We captured him and his fort in less than twenty minutes." The fort fell at about 6:00 p.m., and as Moore noted in his memoir, Lee had surrendered to Grant at Appomattox nine hours before the 117th fought its last battle. The war was over for the McKendree Regiment. During its three years of service, the regiment had marched 2,307 miles in addition to traveling 6,191 miles by water and 778 by rail. It had engaged in six battles and thirty-three skirmishes.

The late Edwin G. Gerling, whose great-grandfather served in the McKendree Regiment, extensively researched the 117th Illinois Infantry and wrote a history of it. He compiled a casualty list that underscores the deadliness of disease at a time when medical science was still in its infancy: 2 men were killed in combat, 9 died of battlefield wounds and no fewer than 109 deaths were attributed to "unknown causes." Gerling's list also noted the deaths of 2 men in prison.

In an address delivered in 1884, Samuel H. Deneen shared a fascinating anecdote about an imprisoned Union soldier who was a "McKendrean," as he proudly observed. Richard Thatcher, the son of a southern Illinois Methodist preacher, was incarcerated in the living hell that was Andersonville prison.

One day, while reading his Bible, Thatcher was accosted by a fellow prisoner, low in stature but with a piercing eye: "What book have you there, my friend?"

"The Bible," was the reply.

"Let me see it. The rebels got mine when they made me a prisoner."

After reading Thatcher's Bible for a while, the other prisoner returned it with words of encouragement that seemed rather strange under the circumstances: "Cheer up, my brother, cheer up. We shall yet find some means of deliverance. God has revealed to me that I am never to die in this rebel prison."

Deneen then revealed the identity of this prisoner: Boston Corbett, who as a member of the 16th New York Cavalry Regiment disregarded orders to take the fugitive John Wilkes Booth alive by shooting him in a Virginia barn on April 26, 1865. Thatcher, who had joined the army at age fifteen, later escaped from Andersonville and eventually reached Union lines.

Risdon Moore moved to Selma, Alabama, after the war and engaged in the coal business until 1875. He relocated to San Antonio, Texas, in 1877, where he worked for the U.S. Treasury. This scholar-warrior died in 1909 and was buried at the San Antonio National Cemetery.

Many Civil War veterans chose to continue their education by enrolling at McKendree College. Some of these young men had incurred serious battlefield injuries. A centennial history of McKendree, issued in 1928, observed that such veterans realized "with the handicap of maimed bodies, it was more necessary to have trained minds in order to succeed in the world's great struggle for the means of livelihood or for success in a business or profession." This history also includes an unforgettable photograph of three such veterans—all of whom had lost their right arms on Southern battlefields. James B. Pinkard, who is seated in the photograph, hailed from Brighton, which is located in the very heart of southwestern Illinois.

The first reunion of 117th Illinois Infantry veterans was an informal event held on the Belleville Fairgrounds in 1888 with about thirty men in attendance. The first organized reunion occurred five years later at Wolf's Grove in Edwardsville and drew forty veterans. Reunions were then held annually, with attendance peaking at seventy-one in 1901 and again reaching that number in 1910. Attendance then began to decline steadily.

The final reunion of the 117th Illinois Infantry was held in 1925. Of the original 985 men who were mustered in on September 19, 1862, only 50 were still alive. Just 6 veterans were able to attend the gathering, and it was decided that there would be no more reunions. Appropriately, this final reunion was held at the birthplace of the 117th Illinois Infantry: McKendree College.

It should be noted that one of McKendree's most celebrated alumni and Union veterans didn't serve in the 117th Infantry. Jacob W. Wilkin enlisted in the 130th Illinois Infantry shortly after his graduation in 1862. Wilkin entered the army as a private but was mustered out as a major. After the war, he became a lawyer and served a total of nineteen years on the Illinois Supreme Court. For two years, he served as its chief justice.

Unlike Shurtleff, McKendree is still very much in existence. It officially became McKendree University in 2007 and offers off-campus classes at several sites, including Scott Air Force Base in St. Clair County.

UNION TOWNS

Elsah

Born in Green County, Kentucky, in 1798, James Semple moved to Edwardsville, the seat of Madison County, Illinois, in 1827 and established a law practice. Just one year later, he won election to the Illinois House of Representatives and proved so adept at politics that he soon became the Speaker of the House. Semple continued his meteoric rise by winning the office of Illinois attorney general in 1833 but failed in his attempt to win a seat in the U.S. Senate three years later. He moved to Alton and used his political connections to obtain the post of Charge d'Affairs to Colombia during the administration of fellow Democrat Martin Van Buren in 1837.

Van Buren was defeated for reelection in 1840 by Whig candidate William Henry Harrison, who died shortly after taking office in 1841 and was succeeded by John Tyler. Even during this interval of Whig ascendancy, Semple managed to keep his diplomatic post until 1842. He then returned to the Prairie State and, upon the election of Judge Sidney Breese to the U.S. Senate, was appointed to fill Breese's seat on the Illinois Supreme Court, where he became chief justice. When Illinois's other U.S. senator, Samuel McRoberts, died in office in 1843, the state legislature elected Semple to succeed him.

Illinois had a powerful voice in the person of James Semple, who strongly championed American expansion into Oregon and supported going to war with Mexico to acquire more territory. This incredibly ambitious man apparently tired of politics and declined to seek reelection to the Senate in 1846. He returned to southwestern Illinois and engaged in real estate. Semple in 1852 purchased some valley acreage that bordered the Mississippi River in Jersey County. The following year, he had the land surveyed for a village he intended to found. Semple constructed a schoolhouse and developed the Elsah Building and Manufacturing Company in 1857. He offered settlers free land with a proviso that required them to purchase all their supplies from him. James Semple was determined to make Elsah a profitable business venture.

Visitors to southwestern Illinois often ask how Elsah acquired its name. Most historians believe that Elsah was derived from Ailsa Crag, a huge rock in the firth of Clyde that would have been the last bit of Scotland that Semple's ancestors saw as they sailed to America in the eighteenth century. A French tourist who visited the village offered another theory regarding the origin of its name. Most of the village's earliest inhabitants came from France and Germany. This tourist believed that some of Elsah's first settlers were German-speaking immigrants from Alsace. The German word for Alsace is *Elsass*, with the double *s* looking like the letter *h* in script, according to the tourist.

Some residents of nineteenth-century southwestern Illinois thought Elsah a peculiar name and called Semple's village Jersey Landing. The settlement was known by both names. It was formally incorporated as Elsah in 1873, seven years after Semple's death.

A fawning biography of Semple written long after his death sang his praises to the heavens: "His every action was dictated by honesty and honor. To him evasions and diplomatic dealings of the underhanded kind were things to be frowned upon and not tolerated by men of character.…He was public spirited, but not for petty purposes, a statesman as contradistinguished from the politician of the present day."

This same biographer assured his readers that Semple's "thoughts were pure, his purposes high and the sunset slope of life found him filled with contentment." The founder of Elsah, who had served in the army during the War of 1812, observed the Civil War "from his quiet homestead overlooking the Father of Waters." Semple was indeed too old to don a uniform for service during that epic struggle. Had he been a bit younger, however, Semple might have taken up arms—but not for the North. James Semple was an active member of the Knights of the Golden Circle and, later, the Sons of Liberty, clandestine organizations that supported slavery and southern independence.

Semple's disloyalty didn't extend to the residents of Elsah, however. The Jersey County community remained staunchly loyal to the North. Its population on the eve of the Civil War was only about 950, but Elsah contributed at least 75 men to the Union army, according to research conducted by Eric Nager. Most of these men were conscripted in late 1864 and early 1865, which means their term of service was brief and they saw limited action; 14 Elsah men, however, were so passionate in their support of the Union that they enlisted in the army in 1861. All 14 served in Company D of the 27th Illinois Volunteer Infantry, which comprised only seven companies and formed on August 10, 1861, at Camp Butler in Springfield under the command of General John A. McClernard; 15 Alton men as well as 6 men from Lamb's Point (as the Madison County town of Worden was then called) also enlisted in Company D.

The 27th Illinois Infantry fought its first engagement on November 7, 1861, at Belmont, Missouri, where it "bore a prominent role and suffered heavily." It was the first Union regiment to land on Island No. 10 during its capture by Shurtleff graduate John Pope. The 27th Illinois participated in the Siege of Corinth, Mississippi, April 29–May 30, 1862, as well as the Siege of Nashville from September 12 to November 6 of that year. Led by John M. Palmer, this battle-hardened unit distinguished itself in the Battle of Stones River, which was fought at Murfreesboro, Tennessee, from December 30, 1862, to January 3, 1863. The regiment remained at Murfreesboro until June.

This unit suffered heavy losses at the Battle of Chickamauga in September 1863. Nager affirmed that the bravery of these Illinois men helped Union general George Henry Thomas earn the nickname the "Rock of Chickamauga." The defeated Union army retreated to Chattanooga, where it was besieged by Confederate forces. The men of Elsah and their Union comrades faced eventual starvation until Brigadier General William Farrar "Baldy" Smith, chief engineer of the Army of the Cumberland, devised the "Cracker Line," a reliable new supply route. The 27th Illinois marched to relieve Knoxville, Tennessee, and participated in the campaign of eastern Tennessee during late 1863 and early 1864.

This proud regiment fought in the Battle of Resaca and the Battle of Adairsville, two engagements of the Atlanta Campaign. It also took part in Siege of Atlanta from July 22 to August 25, 1864. Sherman praised the 27th Illinois's courage under fire by noting that "this gallant regiment performed prodigies of valor" and had even won praise from its battlefield foes. The 27th Illinois was finally relieved from frontline duty on August 25, 1864, when it was ordered to return to Springfield. Its men were mustered out on September 20. Of those fourteen Elsah volunteers, two were dead, three had been wounded, two had been given early discharges for unspecified disabilities and one was missing.

The Elsah veterans helped to make their village a bustling river town in the post–Civil War era. The village served as a vital shipping port for Mississippi River steamboats until the 1890s, when railroads had largely supplanted the river as the preferred means of commercial transportation. Even with the river traffic gone, Elsah thrived. An old business directory for the village noted that the community contained two hotels, three general stores, blacksmith and buggy shops, a cooper shop and many other establishments. Industries included lime-burning and a brickworks, as well as cider- and winemaking. Elsah also had saloons in the nineteenth century. Village residents passed a prohibition ordinance in 1891, which remains in effect to this day.

Trains ran to Elsah only erratically until the Bluff Line Railroad linked it to Alton in 1891. The village was not easily accessible by motorcar until the completion of the Great River Road in 1965. The residents of Elsah cherish their unique and beautiful village. Nearly all the stone and brick buildings date from the years 1853 to 1861 and were built in the Greek Revival style. Buildings in the Franco-American and Gothic Revival styles can also be found in Elsah. The entire village was placed in the National Register of Historic Places in 1973.

Elsah since 1935 has been the site of Principia College, a liberal arts college for Christian Scientists. Acclaimed architect Bernard Maybeck of San Francisco designed the campus to resemble an English village, and it recently received National Landmark status.

ALTON

Located in Madison County on the banks of the Mississippi River, Alton acquired notoriety in 1837 when a proslavery mob murdered the abolitionist newspaper editor Elijah Lovejoy and chucked his printing press into the river, as I detailed in *Abolitionism and the Civil War in Southwestern Illinois*. During the years following Lovejoy's slaying, however, the city became a hotbed of abolitionism and Underground Railroad activity.

Massachusetts expatriates Elijah and Sarah Dimmock purchased what is now the Dunphy Building in 1847 and made it into an Underground Railroad station. Major Charles Hunter, a New York expatriate or native of Kentucky depending on which source one consults, made his way to southwestern Illinois and acquired the old Bates farm from Joseph Meachem in 1818, the year that Illinois was admitted to the Union. Hunter's property was located between two newly founded towns: Lower Alton, laid out by Rufus Easton and established on the Mississippi, and Upper Alton, founded by Meachem and situated up a steep hill so that it wouldn't be menaced by floods. Hunter believed that his settlement could serve as an important junction between the two towns and rival Lower Alton as a river port. He named his community Alton on the River. Hunter and his wife—along with his daughters, sons-in-law and a few other pioneer families—comprised the nucleus of Alton on the River, which soon came to be popularly known as Hunterstown after its ambitious founder.

When Lovejoy and his family moved to Alton from St. Louis, Hunter rented them a house in the community that bore his name. Hunter in 1842 ran for governor of Illinois as the candidate of the Liberty Party, which advocated the abolition of slavery. Thomas Ford, the Democratic candidate, won the race with 46,502 votes. Whig candidate Joseph Duncan polled 39,030 votes, while Hunter ran a very poor third, with only 906 Illinoisans casting their ballots for him. The Liberty Party candidate had captured just 1.05 percent of the total vote. Nonetheless, Illinois abolitionists were encouraged by the fact that Liberty Party presidential candidate James Birney had received only 157 votes in Illinois just two years earlier. Given a chance to cast their ballots for Major Charles Hunter, Illinois antislavery men flocked to the polls to support this southwestern Illinois abolitionist. Hunter also served as a conductor on the Underground Railroad. He died in 1859 on the eve of the Civil War.

Alton men, both white and Black, rallied to the Union banner when the war broke out. Illinois governor Richard Yates in July 1862 urged President Abraham Lincoln to "accept the services of all loyal men," which obviously included Black men. The need for men to battle the Confederacy ultimately trumped any reservations that Washington had regarding opening the ranks of the Union army. Enlistment was slow until Frederick Douglass in March 1863 delivered an address in Rochester, New York, titled "Men of Color to Arms." He urged Black men to view the Civil War as a conflict that would destroy the institution of slavery. Black soldiers served in segregated units that were commanded by white officers.

Some Black Illinoisans journeyed to Massachusetts to enlist in the Massachusetts 54th Infantry, an early Black regiment that included two of Douglass's sons. The 1989 film *Glory* introduced modern Americans to this regiment, which suffered horrendous casualties during an unsuccessful assault on Fort Wagner, South Carolina, in 1863. By the end of the Civil War, the Union army included almost 150 Black regiments and artillery batteries.

The organization of the Illinois-based 29th U.S. Colored Infantry in April 1864 gave Black Illinoisans the opportunity to enlist in their own state. According to a Madison County history, about one hundred men from this county enlisted in the 29th. Seven men named Arbuckle, all related, enlisted in Alton, as did nineteen-year-old John W. Riden, who became a sergeant. Corporal Hiram D. Route, a Missouri slave who had escaped to Illinois, worked for a Dr. Hull of

Illinois governor Richard Yates urged Lincoln to allow Black men to fight in the Union army. *Library of Congress.*

Alton for about a year before enlisting. These men and the other Black recruits knew what they could expect if taken alive by the Rebels. The Confederacy had enacted a law stipulating that captured Black Union troops would be tried as rebellious slaves in kangaroo courts, which would invariably find them guilty and order their execution. Black Union troops could also be sold into slavery, even if they had been free as civilians.

During the same month that the 29th was organized, Confederate troops massacred Black Union soldiers who had surrendered at Fort Pillow, Tennessee. The Confederate press applauded the massacre. "Repeat Fort Pillow," the *Richmond Examiner* urged, "and we will bring the Yankees to their senses." The South felt especially threatened by the Union decision to use Black troops. Another Dixie newspaper stated that it was "a deadly stab…at our institutions themselves, because they know that if we are to yield on this point, to treat black men as the equals of whites, and insurgent slaves as the equivalent of our brave soldiers, the very foundation of slavery would be fatally wounded."

Lewis Martin is the subject of one of the most poignant photographs from the post–Civil War era. He escaped slavery in Arkansas and made his way to the village of Upper Alton, Illinois. Many fugitive slaves chose to journey farther north, perhaps even to Canada, where they couldn't be pursued by Southern slave catchers. Martin might well have lived under the protection of Thaddeus Hurlbut, an ardent abolitionist who had made

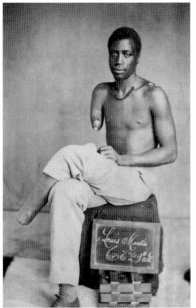
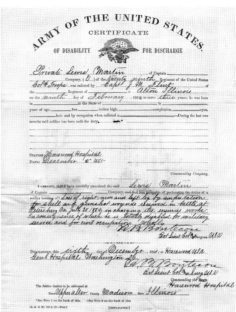

Left: Lewis Martin of Upper Alton was horribly wounded during the Battle of the Crater. *Library of Congress.*

Right: The U.S. Army issued this Certificate of Disability for Lewis Martin. *Library of Congress.*

his Upper Alton home, located where Calvary Baptist Church now stands, into an Underground Railroad station. Nonetheless, Lewis Martin enlisted. Records state that Martin was recruited in Upper Alton to serve in the 29th Regiment Infantry, U.S. Colored Troops, Company E.

Martin incurred the wounds that necessitated the amputation of his left foot and right arm at the disastrous Battle of the Crater in Virginia on July 30, 1864. He was fortunate to have survived this engagement.

After only a few weeks of training, the 29th joined the Army of the Potomac in the late spring of 1864. These brave Illinoisans participated in the Battle of the Crater on July 30, 1864, which occurred during the Siege of Petersburg, Virginia. Union forces tunneled under Confederate lines and planted explosives. When detonated, they would supposedly create a massive breach in the Confederate defenses and allow Union soldiers a point of entry. Black troops, including the 29th, were originally chosen to lead this offensive. At the last moment, however, Union general George Meade decided to use white troops as the initial assault force. He lacked confidence in the fighting ability of Black troops and feared embarrassing the Lincoln administration during an election year by appearing to endanger the lives of Black Americans, according to Edward A. Miller Jr.'s *The Black Civil War Soldiers of Illinois: The Story of the Twenty-Ninth U.S. Colored Troops.*

The explosion indeed created a huge crater that the Black troops had been trained to go around. The white troops who led the assault, however, took cover in the crater and began firing at the enemy. The Confederates quickly encircled the crater and began pouring rifle and artillery rounds down on the Union soldiers in what became a turkey shoot. The 29th and the other Black troops attempted to relieve their white comrades but could do nothing to reverse the disaster. Some Rebels initially fled from the Black troops because, in the words of a Confederate captain, "we could not expect the sons of Southern gentlemen to fight niggers." Other Rebels were outraged at seeing Black Union troops. A Confederate officer conceded that his men "disregarded the rules of warfare which restrained them in battle with their own race, and brained and butchered the blacks until the slaughter was sickening." A Union colonel who emerged from the crater with a Black soldier to surrender recalled the Rebels shouting, "Shoot the nigger, but don't kill the white man!" The colonel was taken prisoner, while the Black soldier was murdered in cold blood.

A white Union officer recalled, "Many a dusky warrior had his brains knocked out with the butt of a musket, or was run through with a bayonet while vainly imploring mercy." Edward Porter Alexander, a Confederate general, noted, "Some of the Negro prisoners who were originally allowed to surrender…were afterward shot."

Research conducted by Kathleen Heyworth indicates that Lewis Martin was granted a disability pension by the U.S. government after the war and lived in Springfield, Illinois. He died in 1892 and was buried as a pauper at that city's Oak Ridge Cemetery. Newspaper articles about this veteran's death were brutally frank. Heyworth found one that sarcastically noted that most of Martin's pension "went to local saloon-keepers."

As a Black man with such horrendous disabilities in the United States of that era, Martin lived a wretched life. He had no family. A headline announcing his death read, "Louis [*sic*] Martin, a Colored Man, Dies Alone."

The obituary of John Hale Sr., a white Union veteran, appeared in the February 10, 1908 edition of the *Alton Evening Telegraph* and was considerably more laudatory. "He was 62 years old," the obituary informed readers, "and he spent nearly all of his life in Alton." Hale "was a good man, a hard working, honest and conscientious man" and left behind a wife and four children. He died at St. Joseph's Hospital following surgery "for relief of a

Left: The grave of Civil War veteran Lewis Martin. *Wikimedia Commons.*

Right: John Hale Sr. is buried at St. Patrick's Catholic Cemetery in Godfrey. *Photo by author.*

malady from which he had been a sufferer for years." Hale's funeral was held at "the cathedral," as Saints Peter and Paul Catholic Church on State Street was then known since it served as the See for the Diocese of Alton.

Hale's obituary contained no information about his Civil War service beyond noting, "When the war broke out he enlisted and served bravely and faithfully until the close." His tombstone notes that Hale served in Company F of the 7th Illinois Infantry. My research revealed that he enlisted on February 21, 1864, and was mustered out on July 9, 1865. Since Hale was just sixty-two at the time of his death in 1908, he would have been about eighteen at the time of his enlistment.

The Illinois 7th was a proud regiment. It was assigned the no. 7 because, according to the Illinois Adjunct General's Report, the Prairie State "sent six regiments to the Mexican war, by courtesy the numbering of the regiments which took part in the war for the Union began with number seven." The report states that recruitment for men to serve in Company F took place in "Bunker Hill and vicinity."

The report also underscored this unit's distinctions. "It will not be improper to say that the Seventh Infantry takes great pride in the fact that it was the first organized regiment from this Stated [*sic*] and mustered into the United States service in the war to save the Union, and the first to return to the capital of the State and re-enlist as veterans." As I am someone who appreciates antique firearms, the report's next assertion really piqued my interest. The 7th was "the only regiment in the whole army that purchased its own guns—the Henry rifle, 16-shooters—paying $50 each for them out of their meager pay of $13 per month, thereby increasing their effective force five-fold." That $50 in 1860 equaled $1,555 in today's money.

The breech-loading, lever-action Henry rifle was a much more effective battlefield weapon than the government-issued muzzle-loading muskets that were carried by most Union troops. The muskets, which took paper cartridges that contained black powder and a lead ball, had to be reloaded after each firing. A fresh percussion cap placed on the musket's nipple ignited the paper cartridge. This cumbersome reloading process limited a musket's rate of fire to just two or three rounds per minute.

Produced by New Haven Arms, the Henry rifle was a formidable weapon for that era. The tubular magazine of a Henry contained sixteen rounds of metallic-cased .44-caliber rimfire ammunition. An article on the website of the company that manufactures modern replicas of this weapon notes, "After an encounter with the 7th Illinois Volunteer Infantry, which had the good fortune to be armed with Henrys, one Confederate officer is credited with the phrase, 'It's a rifle that you could load on Sunday and shoot all week long.'"

The Henry's principal drawback was that its bullet was propelled by just twenty-six to twenty-eight grains of black powder. The Spencer, which was the other repeating rifle that was used by Union forces during the Civil War, fired metallic-cased cartridges loaded into a tubular magazine, which held seven Spencer 56-56 rounds. In the hands of a skilled rifleman, the Spencer could fire up to twenty rounds per minute.

Those Henry rifles of the 7th Illinois Infantry belonged to the men who had purchased them, not the government, and could be brought home when the war ended. We can only speculate what happened to the Henry purchased by John Hale Sr.

Alton resident John Kuhn distinguished himself during the Civil War. Born in Gallen, Switzerland, on May 20, 1833, Kuhn immigrated to the United States and landed in New York in June 1849. He worked as a farm laborer in Pennsylvania during his first summer in America. He later moved to eastern Tennessee, where he spent three years. During this period, according to one who knew him during the Civil War, "he spent three years, part of the time in a glass factory in Knoxville, and part of the time boating on the Tennessee River."

Kuhn moved to Alton in 1854, where he worked in the lumber business and, later, at a bank. He married Catherine Yackel, by whom he had three sons. Kuhn joined the Alton Jaegers in 1855. As I explained in my *Abolitionism and the Civil War in Southwestern Illinois*, the Jaegers were a military unit composed of German immigrants who belonged to Alton's Turnverein, an organization for German Americans. Kuhn's service in the Jaegers gave him invaluable military experience for his service in the Union army during the Civil War. By the time the war began in 1861, Kuhn had risen to the rank of captain. The Alton Jaegers became Company A of the 9th Illinois Volunteer Infantry on July 26, 1861.

Kentucky, although a slaveholding state, remained in the Union. Confederate forces under General Leonidas Polk captured Columbus, Kentucky, on September 3–4, 1861. As John P. Cashon noted in "Paducah— Gateway to the Confederacy," this action posed a threat to the Union since "[t]he bluffs at Columbus dominated the Mississippi below the confluence with the Ohio River." General Grant responded by occupying Paducah. This move gave Grant control of the Ohio, Tennessee and Cumberland Rivers. "After its occupation," Cashon wrote, "Paducah became a staging area for Union troops, a supply depot and hospital center for the care of the sick and wounded." Kuhn on September 9 was appointed the provost marshal of Paducah, and his company was detached to serve as provost guard. Kuhn was promoted to major on December 2, 1861.

The Illinois 9th saw action at Fort Donelson and Shiloh in 1862. The 9th suffered the heaviest losses of any Union regiment at the Battle of Shiloh. Kuhn was the only 9th field officer who wasn't wounded. That November, however, Kuhn suffered a wound at the Battle of Corinth, Mississippi, in 1862. He served as commander of a convalescent camp in Memphis, Tennessee, in the summer and fall of 1863. Kuhn rejoined the regiment at Athens, Alabama, on November 21, 1863, according to Marion Morrison, who served as chaplain of the 9th Illinois and wrote *A History of the Ninth Regiment Illinois Volunteer Infantry*, which was published in 1864.

Born in Ohio in 1823, Morrison became the first professor of mathematics and natural philosophy at Monmouth College when that institution was founded in 1853. Ten years later, at the invitation of a former student, he visited the 9th Illinois Infantry when it was camped in Tennessee. Morrison so impressed the officers that they asked him to serve as the unit's chaplain. Morrison was the great-uncle and namesake of the actor John Wayne.

Kuhn is mentioned by Morrison several times. In a chapter titled "Biographical Sketches of the Field and Staff Officers," he gave a few details about Kuhn's life as a civilian and then offered a brief overview of his career as an officer in the Illinois 9th. In April 1861, Kuhn initially volunteered for just three months but reenlisted for three years, Morrison closed his thumbnail biography of Kuhn by noting that he was "at present writing, he has command of his Regiment, Lieut. Col. [Jesse J.] Phillips being assigned to the command of the mounted forces at Decatur, Alabama."

Neither Kuhn nor Phillips probably were aware that their names were also linked in yet another published work in 1864: the March 30 edition of the *Montgomery (AL) Advertiser*. Their mention in that Dixie newspaper was decidedly unflattering.

"The darkest chapter in the history of this cruel war if not in any other war, will record the atrocities of the Yankees wherever in the Confederate States they have been permitted to march their thieving, brutal hordes," the article began. After comparing the Union armies to Goths and Vandals pillaging Europe, Turks devastating Greece and Russians despoiling Poland, the writer finally settled down enough to give an account of the Illinois 9th's behavior in Limestone County, Alabama. He made a point of noting that the 9th is "commanded by Lieut. Col. Jesse J. Phillips of Belleville, Illinois."

He got it wrong. According to Morrison, Phillips was born in Montgomery County and practiced law in Hillsboro, the county seat, when he enlisted in the army. "In politics," Morrison wrote, "he was a Breckenridge Democrat. Had stumped it, for Breckenridge, in 1860." The Democratic Party split into two in the presidential election of 1860. Northern Democrats supported Senator Stephen Douglas of Illinois, while Southern Democrats nominated Vice President John C. Breckenridge as their presidential candidate. Southern Democrats had never forgiven Douglas for opposing the Lecompton Constitution, which would have brought Kansas into the Union as a slave state. Both Breckenridge and President James Buchanan had strongly supported the Lecompton Constitution. Kansas finally entered the Union as a free state in 1861.

As I pointed out in *Abolitionism and the Civil War in Southwestern Illinois*, Douglas had also angered slavery supporters by a statement he made during a debate with Republican candidate Abraham Lincoln in 1858 for Illinois's U.S. senate seat. Lincoln had asked the Little Giant, as Douglas was called, whether the people of a territory could lawfully exclude slavery prior to the formation of a state constitution. Douglas had replied that slavery could not exist within any territory if the citizens didn't pass the necessary laws to protect slavery. Such an answer made Douglas seem insufficiently supportive of the "peculiar institution" in the eyes of many southerners.

As the presidential candidate of the Southern Democrats, Breckenridge carried every state that would secede from the Union, with the sole exceptions of Tennessee and Virginia. During the Civil War, he served as a major general in the Confederate army and was appointed by Jefferson Davis as secretary of war in February 1865.

Phillips, according to Morrison, "had a strong desire to engage in a military life. When the call was made, he at once went to work to raise a Company…and was elected Captain, April 17th, 1861." Loyalty to the Union clearly trumped Phillips's previous support for a proslavery Democrat who had sided with the Confederacy. Phillips built a distinguished judicial career after the Civil War. He served on the Illinois Supreme Court from 1893 until his death in 1901. Phillips was chief justice in 1897.

The *Montgomery Advertiser* article continued: "On January 25, [Alabama-born] Gen. [Phillip] Roddy [*sic*], with a small portion of his command, attacked the forces of Liet. Col. Phillips, who were encamped near and in the grove of Mrs. Coleman, the widow of Judge Daniel Coleman, deceased." Virginia-born Daniel Coleman (1801–1857) enjoyed a long, distinguished career in Alabama and served on that state's Supreme Court. "As a judge," according to the 1888 work *Northern Alabama: Historical and Biographical Illustrated*, Coleman was "dignified, laborious and impartial," as well as a "conspicuous and zealous member of the Methodist Episcopal Church South." He was a vice-president of the Alabama State Colonization Society, which promoted the emigration of free Blacks to Liberia. "The enemy's pickets were driven into the encampment, when they, with those of the forces who were in camp, took shelter behind the dwelling house of Mrs. Coleman." Elizabeth Peterson Coleman, a native of South Carolina, is praised in that same 1888 work as "noted for beauty of face and character" and "a brilliant conversationalist and noted hostess." She died in 1888. Phillips's men "fired a few rounds" at Roddey's men and then "fled in perfect consternation," *Montgomery Advertiser* gloated.

The article informed readers that "[o]ne of our secret scouts who were in the enemy's lines a day of two after the raid, said that the treatment of Col. Phillips's men to Mrs. Coleman and family was unparalleled in the history of the war." A "secret scout" was a Confederate soldier wearing a Union uniform who infiltrated Union troops to gather information. If apprehended, this Confederate would have been regarded as a prisoner of war. A Confederate spy wearing a Union uniform would be "liable to summary execution," as noted by Mark C. Hageman in his article "Espionage in the Civil War." The newspaper account continued:

Our men having accomplished their purpose, were scarcely out of sight, when the Yankees rushed back to their encampment perfectly infuriated because of their defeat. To avenge themselves, they rushed into the house of Mrs. Coleman with firebrands and built up a fire in one of the handsomest parlors. The mother and daughter implored them not to burn the house, but they heeded not their entreaties. They pushed them violently out of the house drawing pistols on them both.

Kuhn, whose name is misspelled throughout this account, now arrived on the scene:

In a few hours that portion of the command that was on a scout at the time of the attack by Gen. Roddy [sic], *which was commanded by Maj. Kuhne returned to camps. They rushed into the house of Mrs. Coleman and commenced plundering. Mrs. Coleman appealed to Maj. Kuhne to control his men and so give her his protection as a defenseless female. He ordered her from his presence saying, "Woman, go away, I have no protection for you. Men, pitch into her house, and sack it from bottom to top."*

The vandals needed no encouragement from their officer but immediately obeyed to do their work of destruction. Mrs. Coleman had her two little boys, her only protection, she having lost in this cruel war two as noble and as brave sons as any mother had, and her oldest son absent in the services of his country. Her little boys were torn from her in the night and carried to the jail. Their mother pled with the Colonel for their release, when he added to her already unmiterable anguish by saying that he would have to send the older one of the boys to Northern prisons—he however relented in a few days, after torturing their mother sufficiently, as he thought, and released the boys from their imprisonment. Mrs. Coleman and daughter were driven from their home in the night to seek refuge in the town of Athens, which was about one mile distant.

Details such as these indicate that the Coleman family lived well:

The furniture, which was of the finest rosewood, was split up. The marble slabs to the bureaus and wash stands were broken into pieces, mirrors were shattered—handsome Brussels carpets cut up into saddle-blankets, beds dragged out into camp with all the bed clothing, including the finest blankets and Marseilles quilts.

The portrait of Judge Coleman, also that of Mrs. Coleman were so pierced by their bayonets that they could not be recognized. All of the table ware and several pieces of silver were taken out into camp. Several handsome silk dresses and other articles of clothing belonging to the family were taken. A little trunk which Mrs. Coleman prized more than anything else because it contained the mementos and letters of her noble sons who had given their precious lives for their country was broken open, and the precious contents destroyed by their infamous hands. The books of a large and select library were scattered through the camp and destroyed. All of Mrs. Coleman's music was taken. After the completion of their work of destruction, the officers, Major Kuhne and others, took possession of the home and are now quartered in it. Mrs. Coleman, daughter and two sons, were ordered out of the Yankee lines.

This account then noted that these Yankee invaders nonetheless showed Mrs. Coleman a measure of compassion. Due to her poor health, she was allowed to remain in her home. However, the vacate order stood for her three children. "Miss Coleman and her two little brothers are now exiles in our lines."

How accurate is this account? Its author loathed the Yankees who had invaded his state, so he could hardly render an objective report of their activities. One must also keep in mind that he wasn't an eyewitness to these events. Instead, he relied on the accounts of the secret scout. There is undoubtedly some measure of truth in even so biased an article, however. Union troops frequently made use of what they found in Confederate homes, particularly if those homes belonged to well-to-do Southern families. If the Illinois 9th needed saddle blankets, cutting up those "handsome Brussels carpets" would have made sense.

If this incident reflected the worst traits of John Kuhn's character, Morrison's book contains another incident that exemplifies his best. He recorded the following episode in his book to give readers some idea of the horrors of slavery: "During the recent scout to Courtland and Moulton [towns in Lawrence County, Alabama], when in camp near the former place, the orders of Lieut. Col. Phillips were to be ready to move by daylight. The guard were instructed to wake them two hours before day."

Adjutant Henry Klock "was informed by an orderly that there was a lady wishing to see the Colonel." The woman, Morrison tells us, "was very decently, but plainly dressed." By "the Colonel," Morrison is probably referring to Lieutenant Colonel Phillips. The unit's full colonel was August Mersey, who had been born in Germany and resided in Belleville at the beginning of the war. Phillips was duly awakened and informed that a woman wished to see him. "In a half-sleeping condition," as Morrison puts it, the colonel told the adjunct to see what the woman wanted.

When Klock asked why she wanted to speak to the colonel, "He was perfectly amazed by her reply." The woman said that "her master was going to sell her, and she wished to know if she could not go with them." Her plea demonstrates that, despite the Civil War and the threat posed by Union armies in the Confederacy, the sale of slaves continued unabated.

Clearly moved, Klock assured this slave "that he would speak to the Colonel about it, and that he thought they could make arrangements for her to go with us." The well-meaning adjunct was unable to keep his promise, however. "The Colonel having dropped asleep in the meantime, the matter was referred to Major Kuhn." The Alton resident "told her at once that she could go along." The woman, who is never named in Morrison's account, "came into Decatur [Alabama] with our Regiment." He wrote that she "was so nearly white, that she was mistaken for a white woman. She was, in all probability, her master's daughter or sister."

Lincoln's Emancipation Proclamation, which took effect on January 1, 1863, in theory liberated all slaves in states that had joined the Confederacy. In practice, however, the proclamation was simply ignored by Dixie slave-owners. Why should they obey an edict issued by that Yankee president when they were no longer citizens of the United States?

The Union armies that entered the South put teeth into the Emancipation Proclamation, however. Slaveholders could shrug off a Yankee document but not Yankee soldiers such as John Kuhn. The Illinois 9th compiled an admirable record of liberating slaves. According to the website for the Colonel Friedrich K. Hecker Camp no. 443 (https://heckercamp443.org), on May 31, 1863, the 9th raided Florence, Mississippi, and freed more than two hundred slaves.

With the expiration of his term of service with the Illinois 9th, Kuhn returned to Alton and was given command of the Illinois 144th Infantry. History has largely overlooked the Illinois 144th Infantry, however. It engaged in no battles with Confederate soldiers. In fact, its troops never even left the area.

Organized in Alton and mustered into service on October 21, 1864, the Illinois 144th Infantry consisted of nine companies. Companies A and B included a number of men from Alton and Upper Alton, as well as neighboring communities such as Piasa, Brighton and Woodburn. Every man in Company C was from Alton. Even its captain, Augustus DeLange, as well as its first lieutenant, Charles Robideau, and second lieutenant, John Barnard, were Alton residents.

The ruins of the old prison in Alton, where Confederate prisoners of war were incarcerated. *Photo by author.*

If Civil War historians have paid scant attention to the Illinois 144th Infantry, at least part of the blame must be assigned to the unit itself. The Illinois Adjunct General's Report contains much information regarding the Illinois 7th Infantry but little about the 144th Infantry. "Notwithstanding diligent effort was made to obtain historical mention of the services of this Regiment, none was sent into the office and hence it was not in our power to say anything authentic concerning the campaign of the Regiment," it reads.

For information regarding the 144th, one must go to sources such as the website of the Madison County Historical Society. A section of the site titled "Guarding the Alton Prison" states, "Six successive regiments guarded the Alton facility while it functioned as a military prison. The last garrison was composed of the 144th Illinois Infantry." The site notes that James Manchester, a member of Company B, "was on detached service on Smallpox Island for several months." Readers of *Abolitionism and the Civil War in Southwestern Illinois* are familiar with the smallpox epidemic that swept through Alton's military prison and necessitated the creation of an isolation hospital on an island in the Mississippi opposite the prison. The 144th never saw combat, but service in this unit was nonetheless hazardous.

Modern medicine was in its infancy during the Civil War, and the germ theory of disease had not yet been universally accepted. According to the website, 1,159 men served in the Illinois 144th Infantry; 69 lost their lives to infectious diseases such as smallpox, rubella and measles. This was by no means an isolated incident. Twice as many Union troops died from disease as from combat wounds.

Kuhn survived his service with the 144th and was eventually promoted to full colonel. But the man who couldn't be felled by muskets, artillery or germs fell victim to a strange accident not long after the Civil War's conclusion. The circumstances of his death, as reported in the October 27, 1865 edition of the *Alton Daily Telegraph*, shocked the community:

> *Our citizens were astounded on Saturday afternoon by the news of the death of Colonel John H. Kuhn, Alderman from the Third Ward. The facts appear to be that he was engaged during the day in cleaning up the vessels and vats in his brewery, and intending to clean a certain vat, without taking the usual precaution of ventilating it, he put his head through the hole left for such purposes. A man who started to get some water to use in cleansing the vat returned in a minute or two, and noticing him partly in the vat, asked him some question to which he received no reply. He then pulled him out, and he was entirely dead. It is supposed that the gas killed him instantly upon his putting his head through the hole.*

Kuhn had purchased part interest in the brewery, owned by his brother-in-law, after the war. The fact that he had entered local politics demonstrated that he intended to put down roots in Alton. A careless error felled a man who had survived active service during our nation's deadliest war. John Kuhn was just thirty-two.

The long-dead Kuhn drew mention in the May 14, 1879 edition of Alton's newspaper. Emil Guelich of Alton was the regimental surgeon of the Illinois 9th:

> *As we were coming up from St. Louis last evening, on the fast express, in company with Dr. E. Guelich, he beguiled the time in relating some incidents of army life, one of which was a good illustration of how charity is sometimes rewarded.*
>
> *Some twenty years before the war, said the Doctor, the late Col. John Kuhn of Alton, then a boy ten or twelve years old, was on his way to join his parents in East Tennessee. Traveling up the Tennessee River, his funds became exhausted and he was put off the boat at Decatur, Alabama.*
>
> *Wandering up into the town, he sat down on the porch of a hotel kept by a widow woman named McCarty. There he sat forlorn and wretched, without money or friends. The kind hearted landlady saw him crying and asked the cause, whereupon he told his story which aroused her sympathies and she took the friendless boy into the hotel, gave him his meals and lodging, and the next day provided means for him to pursue his journey.*

Mrs. McCarty's kindness to this immigrant youth was rewarded during the Civil War:

> *Twenty years after the incident occurred, the Federal armies were approaching Decatur. In command of the advance column was the same friendless boy above mentioned, at that time Major of the Ninth Illinois. The day before the army occupied the town, Dr. Guelich entered it under a flag of truce and was requested by Maj. Kuhn to ascertain if a Mrs. McCarty still lived there and kept a hotel. On recieving [sic] information that his benefactress was still living, Maj. Kuhn issued strict order to the troops not to molest Mrs. McCarty, or her hotel. Decatur was burned, only one house being left standing, and that was the hotel of widow McCarty.*
>
> *Maj. Kuhn, when he left the place, obtained protection papers for Mrs. McCarty from the Provost Marshall and she drove such a thriving business during the war by means of the privileges obtained for her by the grateful Major that she made a fortune. Such was the return she received after many years for an act of disinterested kindness to a poor boy. Unlike many similar stories which are common in story books, this incident has the merit of being an actual occurrence.*

Guelich's recollection is at odds with an article about Decatur's history on the city's website that states, "By the war's end the city had suffered complete devastation, with all but three buildings burned to the ground." Nonetheless, the McCarty incident demonstrated that even in the hell of war, John Kuhn possessed gratitude and compassion.

Born in 1833—not 1828, as Morrison gives it—in the Duchy of Schleswig in what is now northern Germany, Guelich interrupted his medical studies to serve in the army when the German Confederation went to war with Denmark in 1848. Three years later, he moved to the United States. He resumed his medical studies and graduated from the St. Louis Medical College in 1859. He settled in Alton that same year. In their July 2, 1976 article for the *Telegraph*, Paul Nedde and Ann Perry stated that Guelich's residence, located at the corner of East Fourth and Henry, served as an Underground Railroad station.

When the Civil War broke out, Guelich enlisted for a three-month term in Company K of the Illinois 9th. He reenlisted when his term expired and was promoted to the position of assistant surgeon. Guelich was promoted to chief surgeon on April 28, 1862.

Morrison noted that Guelich began his military service as "a private in the Regiment. One day he was stationed to guard a powder magazine." Guelich "knew a picket should never leave his post until relieved from duty." Morrison informed us that a soldier assigned picket duty serves two hours and then has four hours off during a twenty-four-hour period. "The first two hours passed away, no relief came. Two hours more passed. He supposed that surely at that change he would be relieved. Still no relief came. Another two hours passed. Still no relief."

Guelich wound up serving picket duty for twenty-four consecutive hours without access to food and water. "Another thing which caused the time to pass heavily with him, like almost all Germans, in fact almost all soldiers, he was very fond of his pipe." Guelich dared not to light his pipe while so close to the powder magazine.

After relating this incident, Morrison stated, "There is only one thing, so far as I know, that will cause the Dr. to abandon his proper post. When the Regiment is engaged in battle, unless there is immediate need for him in the rear to care for the wounded, he will leave his post, as a non-combatant, and seeking some position in the advance, he is seen deliberately firing away at the enemy with his revolver." When a Union soldier suffered a wound, "he hastens to the rear to attend to him. That done, and he is off again to his firing-post." Dr. Emil Guelich could be either a healer or killer, depending on the situation.

The Battle of Fort Donelson was fought from February 11 to February 16, 1862. It was a stunning victory for the Union. Morrison recalled that after the battle, Guelich "was placed on board a steamer with 275 wounded men" and then "shoved out into the [Cumberland] river, without any medicine, without anything for the men to eat, with no instruments but carpenter tools." According to Morrison, this nightmare scenario lasted for three days.

"If he attempted to take off a limb, he had to use a common cook's knife for a dissecting knife, and a carpenter's saw to sever the bone." Although both ether and chloroform were in use as anesthetics during the Civil War, neither was available aboard this steamer. One can barely imagine the agony these wounded soldiers endured during amputations.

"He had no bandages with which to wrap up the wounds, except he take the only shirt they had." Morrison demonstrated his penchant for understatement with the observation, "This truly was a trying position in which to place a good surgeon."

Guelich returned to Alton after the war and resumed his medical practice. He died in 1893. His biography in *Centennial History of Madison*

County noted that Guelich was a staunch Republican and that "it was one of his greatest pleasures to throw himself and his influence into a political campaign, always choosing the place where the fight was the hottest." His *Telegraph* obituary stated, "His kindness of heart and his generosity made him the friend of rich and poor."

BUNKER HILL

For historically literate Americans, the name Bunker Hill immediately brings to mind a battle of the American Revolution. For southwestern Illinoisans, however, Bunker Hill also refers to a small town in southern Macoupin County that has one of the most impressive statues of Abraham Lincoln in the nation. Residents justifiably take pride in the knowledge that their community received this statue as a tribute to the men of Bunker Hill, who rallied to the Union banner during the Civil War.

When Lincoln issued his call for volunteers to enlist in the Union army, Illinois reached its assigned quota so quickly that many men had to be turned away. Determined to fight for the North, these men journeyed to other states where enlistment quotas had not yet been met. A number of men from Bunker Hill, Carlinville and several neighboring communities joined Company B of the 1st Missouri Volunteer Cavalry, which was organized by Captain Charles Clinton of St. Louis at Jefferson Barracks, Missouri, on August 1, 1861. A Massachusetts native and former schoolteacher, Clinton was working for a St. Louis brokerage firm when the war broke out. He immediately resigned and obtained a commission as a captain in the Union army. Clinton's grandfather held the rank of captain during the American Revolution, and he took pride in serving the nation that his ancestor had helped to bring into existence.

Company B served principally in southern Missouri and Arkansas. The late Carl Stanton, who conducted extensive research into the history of Macoupin County, identified at least eighty men from the Greater Bunker Hill area who served in Company B. The names of these men, their ranks and brief summations of their service records can be accessed on the website Missouri Digital Record: Soldiers' Records, War of 1812—World War I.

Benjamin Green of Carlinville, who was mustered in as a second lieutenant, had risen to the rank of captain by the end of the war. Mustered in as a first lieutenant, Elisha Williams of Bunker Hill made captain in

1863. Their military careers stand in stark contrast to that of Corporal George Adams, who was denied the opportunity to display his mettle on a Civil War battlefield. This Bunker Hill native enlisted on August 5, 1861, and died in a St. Louis hospital on September 1 of that year. The poignancy of his fate is matched by that of Private William Alexander, who met death not on a battlefield or even in a hospital. He died in Bunker Hill while at home on furlough.

As previously stated, the Union army lost twice as many men to disease than combat. This grim fact was corroborated by Stanton's research into Company B. Philander Nesbit, Henry Weick, George Link and several others are listed as having died in hospitals. Some men were granted early discharges for unspecified reasons, and a few deserted. Private Thomas Denby's military career is noteworthy for its brevity. He enlisted on August 13, 1861, was mustered in at Jefferson Barracks, Missouri, on September 6 and deserted three days later while still at Jefferson Barracks. Denby died in a St. Louis hospital in November of that year.

Joseph Bena's indecisiveness rivaled that of Hamlet. This bugler who deserted at Springfield, Missouri, in July 1862 evidently had a change of heart and then returned to Company B in June 1863. Just two months later, however, Bena concluded that he was finished with the Union army once and for all and again deserted while Company B was at Duvall's Bluff, Arkansas. Two desertions by the same soldier—and occurring in different states—could well be a Civil War record.

Most of Company B's battlefield casualties occurred during the charge at Sugar Creek, Arkansas, on February 17, 1862. Officially known as the Skirmish at Little Sugar Creek, the engagement occurred when Union forces under Brigadier General Samuel R. Curtis attacked three regiments under the command of Confederate colonel Louis Hébert, which were covering the retreat of Confederate general Sterling Price. The 1st Missouri Cavalry led the Union charge down Telegraph Road, taking heavy fire from a Confederate battery. In his official report about the engagement, Curtis stated, "After a few rounds of shot and shell I ordered a cavalry charge, which drove them [the Confederates] from the high ground they occupied, with the loss of many killed, wounded and scattered. My loss is 13 killed and 20 wounded."

Among those killed were Corporal Franklin Carr and Private James Carrico, both from Carlinville. Sergeant George McPherson of Bunker Hill and Private James Smith of Carlinville were wounded and later discharged for disabilities. The skirmish at Little Sugar Creek marked the first time that the Confederate battle flag was flown in the Trans-Mississippi Theater of the war, as well as the first significant engagement fought in Arkansas.

According to Stanton's research, the last member of Company B to die in combat was William Singler, a bugler, who was wounded on an Arkansas road on November 17, 1863, and died four days later. Like so many other men who volunteered to serve in this unit, Singler lived in Bunker Hill.

Charles Clinton resigned his commission on January 9, 1863. He moved to New Orleans after the Civil War to manage a shipping company and was later appointed to the post of superintendent of the U.S. Mint in the Crescent City by President Ulysses S. Grant. Clinton entered politics during the Reconstruction era, but with less than stellar results. He was elected the state auditor of Louisiana in 1872 but was impeached for issuing "illegal warrants." Although the state legislature failed to convict him, Clinton's legal troubles continued, and he was tried in a civil court on the same charge. The trial resulted in a hung jury, but Clinton realized that his reputation in Louisiana had been fatally tarnished. He resigned as auditor and moved to Cincinnati.

Clinton had long wanted to do something to honor the Bunker Hill men he had commanded during the war. He consulted Mrs. Moses True, the widow of one of the town's founders, and decided that a statue of our nation's Civil War president would be the most fitting memorial. William Granville Hastings, an English artist, cast the nine-foot bronze statue of Lincoln, which Clinton purchased and donated. Local residents financed the monument's granite base through private subscriptions. One of the monument's two plaques notes the dates of Lincoln's birth and death. The other plaque bears this inscription:

> *1904*
> *In Ever Lasting Memory of*
> *The Conflict By Which The Union*
> *Was Preserved and In Which They*
> *Took Part, This Statue of*
> *Abraham Lincoln*
> *Was Presented To*
> *The Citizens of Bunker Hill*
> *By the Soldiers of Company "B"*
> *Of the First Missouri Cavalry*
> *Charles Clinton, Captain*

The monument was formally unveiled on September 7, 1904, before a crowd of about seven thousand. While Clinton and any number of politicians and local dignitaries were present, the true guests of honor were nine veterans of Company B who still lived in the area and were able to attend this event: John Brandenburger, Bunker Hill; Fred Dabel, Bunker Hill; John Dennison, Carlinville; Herman Heuer, Dorsey; August Kardel, Upper Alton; James Lawrence, Carlinville; James Pocklington, Carlinville; James G. Rumbolz, Bunker Hill; and E.S. Williams, Bunker Hill.

Without their enlistment in that cavalry unit, there would have been no monument in Bunker Hill. Without their patriotism—and the patriotism of the 2.2 million men who fought for the North—the Union would not have been saved and slavery would not have been abolished.

SOUTHWESTERN ILLINOIS MEN
WHO MERIT RECOGNITION

Edward L. Hager: Drummer Boy of Shiloh

Music played a vital role for both the North and South. Rebel soldiers made "Dixie" the unofficial anthem of the Confederacy despite the fact that the song was written by an Ohioan. "The Bonnie Blue Flag" was a favorite marching song of the Rebel armies. Its lyrics included lines that succinctly revealed the cornerstone of the Confederacy:

> *We are a band of brothers native to the soil,*
> *Fighting for the property we gained by honest toil.*

The "property" in question was slaves, which Southerners regarded as possessions rather than human beings.

"The Battle Cry of Freedom," one of the most popular songs of the Union army, explicitly condemned slavery. Written by George Root in 1862 after Lincoln issued a call for 300,000 volunteers for the Union army, "The Battle Cry of Freedom" is historically significant because it contains an endorsement of abolitionism. One stanza goes:

> *We will welcome to our number the loyal, true and brave*
> *Shouting the battle cry of freedom;*
> *And although they may be poor, not a man shall be a slave,*
> *Shouting the battle cry of freedom.*

In other words, the Union army would welcome "the loyal, true and brave" regardless of race. As previously stated, the Union indeed accepted Black recruits for service in units. "Not a man shall be a slave" meant that a Union victory would destroy slavery. That promise implied in "The Battle Cry of Freedom" was partially realized on January 1, 1863, when Lincoln's Emancipation Proclamation freed all slaves held in Confederate states. Freedom's battle cry resounded across the entire United States in 1865 when the Thirteenth Amendment, written and sponsored in the U.S. Senate by longtime Alton resident Lyman Trumbull, forever abolished slavery in our nation.

Other popular Union marching songs included "John Brown's Body," which commemorated the martyred abolitionist who had been hanged for trying to instigate a slave revolt, and "The Battle Hymn of the Republic," which was written by Julia Ward Howe and sung to the tune of "John Brown's Body." Some songs were more suited to being sung by soldiers gathered around a campfire, such as "Tenting Tonight on the Old Campground," an 1863 work by Walter Kittridge. A melancholy song, the lyrics express the anguish felt by the troops who so keenly miss their loved ones at home. The song also laments fallen fellow soldiers with stanzas such as:

> *Alas for the comrades of days gone by*
> *Whose forms are missed tonight.*
> *Alas for the young and true who lie*
> *Where the battle flag braved the fight.*

The carnage of the Battle of Shiloh, fought in southwestern Tennessee on April 6–7, 1862, horrified both the North and South. Although technically a Union victory, the North actually incurred more casualties than the South—13,047 compared to 10,699 for the Confederates. The battle received its name from the Shiloh Methodist Church, which was located near the battlefield. Ironically, the Hebrew word *Shiloh* means "place of peace." William Hays, a prolific songwriter of that era, wrote a ballad later that year titled "The Drummer Boy of Shiloh," which commemorated a Union drummer boy who was fatally wounded. Here are the lyrics:

> *On Shiloh's dark and bloody ground*
> *The dead and wounded lay,*
> *Among them was a drummer boy*

Who beat the drums that day.
A wounded soldier held him up
His drum was by his side;
He clasped his hands, then raised his eyes
And prayed before he died.
He clasped his hands, then raised his eyes
And prayed before he died.

"Look down upon the battle field,
Oh, Thou Heavenly Friend!
Have mercy on our sinful souls!"
The soldiers cried, "Amen!"
For gathered 'round a little group,
Each brave man knelt and cried.
They listened to the drummer boy
Who prayed before he died.
They listened to the drummer boy
Who prayed before he died.

"Oh, mother," said the dying boy,
"Look down from heaven on me,
Receive me to thy fond embrace—
Oh, take me home to thee.
I've loved my country as my God;
To serve them both I've tried."
He smiled, shook hands—death seized the boy
Who prayed before he died.

Each soldier wept, then, like a child,
Stout hearts they were, and brave;
The flag his winding sheet, God's book
The key unto his grave.
They wrote upon a simple board
These words: "This is a guide
To those who'd mourn the drummer boy
Who prayed before he died;
To those who'd mourn the drummer boy
Who prayed before he died.

Ye angels 'round the Throne of Grace,
Look down upon the braves
Who fought and died on Shiloh's plain,
Now slumb'ring in their graves;
How many homes made desolate?
How many hearts have sighed?
How many, like that drummer boy,
Have prayed before they died;
How many like that drummer boy,
Who prayed before they died!

The song became incredibly popular in the North. The drummer's boy fame even outlasted the Civil War. *The Drummer Boy: Or, the Battle-Field of Shiloh, A New Military Allegory in Five Parts*, a production described as "a pleasing mixture of drama, pathos and comedy," was written by Samuel J. Muscroft in 1870. It proved to be such a crowd-pleaser that it was staged in all the northern states for the next forty years.

Curiously, any number of Union veterans stepped forward after the war to claim that they had been the drummer boy. Their desire for fame evidently blinded them to the fact that the Shiloh drummer boy of Hays's song had been killed during the battle. Residents of southwestern Illinois, however, proudly claim the Drummer Boy of Shiloh as one of their own.

Born and raised in White Hall, a small village in Greene County, fourteen-year-old Edward L. Hager followed some soldiers to Greene County's Camp Carrollton and tried to enlist in the 61st Illinois Infantry, which was organized by Colonel Jacob Fry on February 5, 1862. Turned down because of his youth, the undeterred Hager followed the 61st to Benton Barracks in St. Louis. The 61st, which had consisted of just three companies, soon recruited enough men to form nine full companies. One of these new recruits was Hager, who was finally allowed to join the regimental fife and drum corps.

Captain George B. Hanks, Hager's commanding officer at Shiloh, wrote a memoir of this young patriot after the war. As Union casualties mounted during the battle, Hanks recalled, "every musician threw down his instrument" and grabbed a musket that had been dropped by one of the Union dead. Hager was no exception. Hanks was awed by the boy's courage. "All day long we would charge and fall back," he wrote. "It was hard to keep this lad in line. He was ready to charge but hard to make fall back."

Hanks remembered one retreat in particular when Hager ignored the order to fall back. "Just a minute," the boy said. "There's a fellow on a gray

Fourteen-year-old
Edward L. Hager
died from a wound
he received during
the Battle of Shiloh.
Photo by author.

horse over there in that thicket, and if he should show his head again, I would give him a scare." According to Hanks, "at that instant a commanding officer of the gray [Confederate army] threw up his hands and a riderless horse came out of that thicket."

Hager didn't die at Shiloh while surrounded by weeping soldiers, followed by being wrapped in the flag and buried with a Bible. Hanks's account, however, confirmed that Hager was seriously wounded during the battle. The boy "with many others, was placed on a transport boat, sent back north, and I never saw him again." The primitive medicine of that era couldn't save Hager's life. He died in his home on May 30, 1862, at the age of fourteen years, nine months and twenty-six days. This courageous Unionist was buried at White Hall's Lamborn Cemetery, which is also known as the VFW Cemetery.

Was Hager indeed the celebrated Drummer Boy of Shiloh? The administration of the Shiloh National Military Park believes that Hays's song "is undoubtedly based upon fancy rather than fact." Songs with lyrics intended to move listeners to tears were a staple of nineteenth-century popular culture. Still, Hager's fame isn't dependent on whether he inspired a song that most contemporary Americans have never even heard. A fourteen-year-old boy whose love for the Union compelled him to join the army and put his life on the line demands the admiration of every American.

J.R. Miles

J.R. Miles recruited local men to join a unit that was mustered in as Company F of the 27th Illinois Infantry. *Library of Congress.*

A sign on Illinois Route 267 indicates the exit for Miles Station. One follows a road flanked by fields of corn and soybeans to this hamlet, which consists of a few houses and a large cemetery. A tombstone-style marker informs visitors that Miles Station Cemetery was established in 1866.

The cemetery's grass is neatly mowed, and an American flag flies from a large pole. Nonetheless, Miles Station Cemetery is showing its age. Many of the inscriptions on the oldest tombstones are now illegible. One such tombstone marks the grave of a child. I know this because I was able to discern the faint image of a lamb, an animal that symbolizes innocence and was frequently carved on children's tombstones. The monument that marks the graves of Jonathan Miles, founder of Miles Station, and his wife, Elizabeth, remains in splendid condition, however.

Born in 1817 in Kentucky, Miles came to Illinois with his parents, both of whom were southerners by birth. The family in 1832 settled in Macoupin County, where they became "pioneers of Brighton Township," according to the 1891 work *Portrait and Biographical Record of Macoupin County, Illinois.* Macoupin County was quite the wilderness when the Miles family arrived. Jonathan Miles could "remember when there were no roads here, there being an unbroken prairie over which one could ride for miles without fence or house intercepting his progress. Jerseyville, Alton and Carlinville were all then mere hamlets and it often required a week to make a trip to mill."

History of Macoupin County, published in 1879, noted that Miles "attended school some little time in Kentucky" and "had the benefit of instruction for a short period" at an early school in Alton. Miles was largely self-educated or, as the author conceded in nineteenth-century prose, "for his acquirements in the way of an English education, he is mostly indebted to his own efforts." An "English education" was an old term for basic schooling that taught one to read and write.

Miles built the first mill in this part of the county, which proved a boon for area farmers. Miles Station was originally called Providence and later renamed Miles Station to honor its founder. It was indeed a "station" for the

Chicago and Alton Railroad, whose owners Miles convinced to run a line through his settlement. The author praised Miles's character: "His business relations have never been tainted by a suspicion of dishonesty" and "as a man and a citizen," Miles, who belonged to his community's Methodist church, stood "above reproach."

Like Lincoln, Miles was a Whig until that party's collapse. He then became a Republican and remained so for the rest of his life. Whether he and the community he founded played any role in the Underground Railroad has yet to be determined.

When the Civil War broke out, Miles's southern roots in no way deterred his allegiance to the Union. He recruited local men to join a unit that, on August 9, 1861 was mustered in as Company F of the 27th Illinois Infantry. The company roster shows that no fewer than twelve men gave "Miles' [*sic*] Station" as their residence. Men from neighboring communities such as Brighton, Shipman, Plainview, Piasa, Woodburn and Fidelity also joined Company F. This company included fourteen volunteers from Upper Alton and twenty from Alton. Like so many other Illinois units, these men trained at Camp Butler. Miles entered the army as a captain and eventually rose to the rank of colonel.

Company F first saw action in Belmont, Missouri, and later participated in the capture of Confederate-held Island No. 10 in the Mississippi River. Miles led his men through major campaigns such as Missionary Ridge and Chickamauga. "His men conducted themselves with credit," *Portrait and Biographical Record* stated, "reflecting honor upon their commander and his tactics." The company roster recorded only two desertions and one dishonorable discharge. The other men in Company F indeed demonstrated honor and courage.

Henry Adam and John Richardson, both of Shipman, were killed at Missionary Ridge on November 25, 1863. Andrew Pfifer of Columbus, Ohio, fell at Stones River on New Year's Eve 1862. Style Shives of Alton was killed at Peach Tree Creek in Fulton County, Georgia, on July 20, 1864. Several other men died of unspecified causes. At least ten men were wounded, including Leonard Cook of Upper Alton, who was mustered out after being wounded twice—once at Stone River and again during the battle at Rocky Face Ridge, which occurred during Sherman's Atlanta campaign.

Miles led a charmed life on the battlefield. At Chickamauga, according to the 1891 work, "his field glass and sword handle were shot off and his horse was shot out under him." Although "his clothes were several times pierced by bullets," he was never wounded. The work also noted that Miles "never succumbed to sickness." That in itself was quite a feat when one considers that twice as many Union troops died from disease as from combat wounds.

For reasons that remain unclear, Miles resigned his commission while stationed at Cleveland, Tennessee. The 1879 work stated that it was "less than 90 days before the expiration of his three year term of service." The author speculated that his decision to resign was "perhaps connected with his business and his family requiring his immediate presence in Illinois."

Miles Station Cemetery is the final resting place of J.R. Miles, the community's founder. *Photo by author.*

While Miles deserves admiration as an area pioneer who fought for the Union, he also merits respect for the magnanimity he showed a former enemy. Miles met Bushrod Johnson in St. Louis, when the ex-Confederate general was down on his luck as well as a widower with a disabled son, and invited Johnson to move to Miles Station. His bravery as a soldier was matched by his benevolence as a veteran.

Johnson resided in Miles Station from 1875 until his death five years later. He was buried in that community's cemetery, and there he remained—until 1975, when his body was disinterred and sent to Nashville for reburial in the cemetery where his wife rests.

It seems unlikely that anyone who took part in the Underground Railroad would ever repudiate abolitionism. It seems even less likely that anyone who had helped fugitive slaves achieve freedom would fight for the Confederacy. Bushrod Johnson, however, was such a person.

Bushrod Rust Johnson was born into a family of Ohio Quakers on October 7, 1817. Quakers were opposed to slavery on principle, but the Johnsons actively expressed their opposition to the "peculiar institution" by participation in the Underground Railroad. In *Yankee Quaker Confederate General*, his 1971 biography of Johnson, Charles M. Cummings wrote that Nathan Johnson, Bushrod's brother, was born in 1794, taught school, became a physician and actively took part in the abolitionist movement. The age difference between the two brothers meant that Nathan was a second father to Bushrod and played a significant role in his life.

Cummings wrote that young Bushrod attended Quaker meetings where he heard slavery condemned. Nathan's home served as an Underground Railroad station. Fugitive slaves arrived at night, hidden in a secure location such as the cellar or barn, were given food and then spirited away the next night to another station. Nathan's sons assisted him—and so did Bushrod.

Bushrod obtained an appointment to West Point in 1836. Choosing an army career violated the central tenets of his Quaker faith. However, a few other Quakers have served in the military. Paul Douglas, who represented Illinois in the U.S. Senate from 1949 to 1967, converted to the Quaker faith as an adult. However, at age fifty he joined the Marine Corps and fought in World War II. Richard Nixon was born into a Quaker family but sought and received a commission in the U.S. Navy during World War II.

Following graduation from West Point, Johnson was stationed in Florida during the Seminole War. He saw extensive combat during the Mexican-American War. His obituary, published in the September 16, 1880 edition of the *Alton Telegraph*, informed readers that at the end of the war "he resigned and located in Nashville as a professor of a military institute." The truth is more complex and less laudatory. Before the war had even ended, Johnson resigned from the army after disgracing himself by attempting to sell government property for personal profit.

Johnson reinvented himself and taught at the Western Military Institute in Kentucky and the University of Nashville. When the Civil War broke out, Johnson chose to fight for the South and rose to the rank of major general. Cummings suggested that his decision was motivated by financial considerations. By 1860, this ex-Quaker owned $5,000 in Nashville real estate and $12,000 in personal property. He owned almost three times as much property in the South as he owned in the North. Dixie had made Bushrod the wealthiest person in his family, Cummings observed.

The grave marker of J.R. Miles at Miles Station Cemetery. *Photo by author.*

The *Telegraph* obituary noted that Johnson fought in "many of the most important battles" and returned to teaching after the war. A widower with a disabled son, he abandoned Tennessee for St. Louis in 1874, where he entered a commission business.

A letter written by Charlotte Roady, published in the *Telegraph*'s August 15, 1975 edition, described Johnson's life at Miles

Station. Roady wrote that Johnson "made his living cutting hedge posts" and "was loved by the people in the community and always willing to help raise a barn and even helped to build our little church which stood in the center of the cemetery." Roady's grandfather told her that Johnson "was a highly cultured man and had brought his library of books, which he would lend to anyone who wanted to read them."

Miles and Johnson evidently became fast friends. A 1932 Memorial Day newspaper article stated, "At one time Col. Miles of the Union army and Gen. Bushrod Johnson, Confederate, were in the habit of sitting under the church yard trees and talking over the war in which they had served on opposite sides. It is under these same trees where they sleep now." A brief Memorial Day service was held at the Miles Station Cemetery, which included a salute fired over Miles's grave and the playing of taps. A local minister "gave a short talk and Irene Meyers recited Edgar Guest's poem 'Decoration Day.'"

Jonathan Miles died in 1903. The *Alton Evening Telegraph*, which mistakenly gave his place of burial as the nearby town of Shipman, noted, "An old bugler in Col. Miles regiment, who was a personal friend of Col. Miles, will be at the funeral to sound the bugle call of taps." The newspaper also mentioned that Major Frank Moore would serve as one of the honorary pallbearers. We can only speculate whether the conversations between Miles and Johnson also included accounts of participation in the Underground Railroad and whether the old Confederate general ever expressed regret for abandoning abolitionism.

LEANDER STILLWELL

Born in 1843 "in a little old log house" on his family's farm at Otter Creek in Jersey County, Illinois, Leander Stillwell wrote a memoir for his youngest son, who had requested that his father write an account of his years in Company D of the 61st Illinois Volunteer Infantry. The dedication to Jeremiah E. Stillwell is dated July 3, 1916. In the book's preface, the old veteran stated that he made "no pretensions of being a 'literary' man" and that the memoir "is simply the story of a common soldier who served in the army during the great war, and who faithfully tried to do his duty."

His reference to the Civil War as "the great war" is surprising. I had never before seen that term applied to the conflict that tore the United States asunder. Perhaps Stillwell had read newspaper accounts of the conflict we now call World War I, then in progress, when he was writing his memoir. World War I was sometimes referred to as the "Great War," and Stillwell could have unconsciously incorporated the expression in his manuscript. "If this manuscript should ever be published," he wrote, "it will go to the world without any apology or commendation from me whatever."

Stillwell didn't immediately enlist in the Union army when the war broke out because of "the belief then…almost universal throughout the North that the 'war' would amount to nothing more than a summer frolic, and would be over by the 4th of July." While conceding that the Union defeat at the Battle of Bull Run was a "crushing disappointment," Stillwell informed readers that the Confederate victory "was probably for the best" because had Bull Run "been a Union victory and the Rebellion then been crushed, negro slavery would have been retained and the 'irrepressible conflict' would have been fought out likely in your [his son's] time, with doubtless tenfold the loss of life and limb that ensued in the war of the sixties." Neo-Confederates and other Old South apologists claim that slavery wasn't the cause of the Civil War. Stillwell, who lived and fought during those tumultuous times, obviously believed otherwise.

Stillwell's use of the term "irrepressible conflict" indicated that he was familiar with a celebrated and controversial October 25, 1858 address delivered by William Seward, an ardent foe of slavery who later served as Lincoln's secretary of state. Seward stated that the existence of free states and slave states created "an irrepressible conflict between opposing and enduring forces, and it means that the United States must and will, sooner or later, become either entirely a slaveholding nation, or entirely a free-labor nation." The sentiment expressed in Seward's speech is not dissimilar from Lincoln's "House Divided" speech, which was delivered on June 16, 1858.

We learn from Stillwell that southwestern Illinois was by no means solidly pro-Union. "The various counties in that immediate locality were overwhelmingly Democratic in politics, and many of the people were strong 'Southern sympathizers,' as they were then called, and who later developed into virulent Copperheads and Knights of the Golden Circle," he wrote. Copperheads were Northerners who fiercely opposed the Civil War and urged an immediate negotiated peace with the South, even if it meant the recognition of an independent Confederate States of America. As mentioned earlier, Elsah founder James Semple was a member of the Knights of the Golden Circle, later renamed the Sons of Liberty. This clandestine organization of radical Copperheads supported the South and sought to undermine the Union's war effort by engaging in acts of sabotage and encouraging the desertion of Union soldiers. Stillwell was correct in asserting that these traitors to the Union maintained a strong presence in southwestern Illinois, particularly in Jersey County.

The issues that brought about the Civil War split the nation along reasonably well-defined geographic lines. However, as Stephen Z. Starr and other historians have pointed out, it is erroneous to assume that the entire population of the North supported one set of positions on these issues while everyone in the South supported the opposite set of positions. Eastern Tennessee and western Virginia, for example, strongly opposed secession and remained loyal to the Union during the Civil War. Many Northern residents who belonged to the Democratic Party, such as those southwestern Illinois residents to whom Stillwell referred, detested Lincoln for what they saw as his willingness to drag the nation into a conflict at the behest of abolitionists, who were determined to shed the blood of white men in order to end slavery.

The Old Northwest—which comprised the states of Illinois, Wisconsin, Michigan, Ohio and Indiana—became a breeding ground for Copperheads. According to the 1860 census, about 475,000 residents of Illinois, Indiana and Ohio were born in slave states. It has been estimated that no less than 40 percent of the residents of the Old Northwest could claim southern birth or parentage. Such a significant voting bloc ensured that the Democratic Party of Illinois and the other states of the Old Northwest, particularly Indiana and Ohio, would sympathize with the South and oppose any military effort to crush the rebellion. These expatriate southerners wanted an immediate negotiated peace to end the conflict.

Copperheads indeed formed a strong presence in southwestern Illinois, particularly after so many loyal Unionists left the region to serve in the Northern armies. When Bushwhackers were tried for burning a barn and flour mill and the attempted murder of a Unionist in the Randolph County town of Chester, they were quickly acquitted by juries packed with Copperheads. In his Civil War memoir, Stillwell recalled the extent of Copperhead strength in southwestern Illinois:

> *Probably 90 per cent of the inhabitants of Greene, Jersey, Scott, Morgan and adjoining counties came from the Southern States, or were the direct descendants of people from that part of the country. Kentuckians, Tennesseans, and North and South Carolinians were especially numerous. But is only fair and the truth to say that many of the most prominent and*

dangerous of this Copperhead element were men from remote Eastern states. What caused these persons to pursue this shameful course I do not know.

While the Democratic Party provided a political vehicle for Illinois Copperheads to express their opposition to the war, the most fanatical Southern sympathizers needed a clandestine organization that would engage in blatantly illegal activities to undermine the Union cause and ensure a Rebel victory. The Knights of the Golden Circle (KGC) fulfilled that need.

Founded in the 1850s by Virginia native George Washington Lamb Bickley, members of the KGC passionately supported the expansion of slavery in the Western Hemisphere, particularly in Latin American nations and the islands of the Caribbean. Historian Bethania Meradith Smith believed that the genesis of the Knights of the Golden Circle can be found in the numerous Southern Rights Clubs of the 1830s and 1840s. A pamphlet published in Indianapolis in 1861 claimed that these clubs outfitted and sent out six ships for "blackbirding"—a jaunty euphemism for capturing Black people for slavery—between 1834 and 1840. Proslavery zealots flocked to the KGC, which by 1860 claimed a total membership of sixty-five thousand. Members were organized into local units called "castles," since these men took such pride in possessing the title of knights. The organization was strongest in the South but maintained a formidable presence in Illinois, Indiana and Ohio among residents with Dixie roots.

Bickley selected Mexico as the first nation that would fall to the KGC and began making plans for an invasion that would topple the Mexican government and install a proslavery regime. The invasion was scheduled for September 1860 but, plagued by lack of funds and insufficient volunteers, never occurred. Undaunted, Brickley then announced that the KGC would now devote itself to championing the cause of Southern secession. When the Civil War began, the KGC castles in states such as Illinois began a campaign to sabotage the Union's war effort.

The Illinois KGC was dealt a crippling blow by the *Chicago Tribune* when it published a lengthy article in its August 26, 1862 edition that exposed the organization's aims. After noting that a number of prominent Southern Illinoisans, including judges and a former congressman, had just been arrested for treason, the reporter revealed the extent of KGC activity in the Prairie State. He then quoted the deposition of a witness who had returned to the Prairie State after living in the Confederacy.

This witness stated that he was a former Illinoisan who made his home in Alabama and served in the Home Guard of that state for three months. He was mustered out and ordered to enlist in the Confederate army, but with "the assistance of the secret signs of the Knights of the Golden Circle," he was able to travel through the Confederate states until reaching the federal lines at Cairo, Illinois, in May 1862. After settling in Perry County, he was approached by some men who identified themselves as members of the Knights of the Golden Circle. They informed him that the KGC was numerically strong in southwestern Illinois and held meetings every Thursday on Paradise Prairie in Jersey County.

So named because many of its early settlers came from New Jersey, this county epitomized Lincoln's metaphor of the United States as a house divided. Even while a KGC stronghold, Jersey County sheltered several Underground Railroad stations, including the Red House (now known as the Cheney Mansion) in Jerseyville, where fugitive slaves were hidden in a false cellar. Jerseyville was also the residence of George Burke, a Vermont native who came to Jersey County in 1837—the year that Lovejoy was murdered. Describing himself as an abolitionist from religious conviction, he resigned his membership in Jerseyville's proslavery Presbyterian church and founded a Congregational church that opposed slavery.

Burke made his house a station on the Underground Railroad. His obituary in the April 2, 1893 edition of the *Jerseyville Republican* noted that the fugitive slaves from Missouri who found their way to Burke's home crossed the Mississippi River and entered Illinois at Jersey Landing, the Mississippi River village founded by KGC member James Semple.

The *Tribune*'s informant attended the KGC meeting, which was held "on an uncultivated field near the residence of W.M.A. Haines" in Paradise Prairie. Armed guards were stationed around the field to ward off intruders. Besides Haines, about seventy other KGC members were in attendance. According to the informant, "The members dress themselves in a cheap uniform which they had prepared consisting of white pants with a red stripe up the outside of the leg, and blue coat with white and red stripes over the arm and back." Despite their red, white and blue attire, these men were hardly patriots. Their avowed goal was to aid the Confederacy, which was underscored by the reading of a letter purported to be indirectly from Jefferson Davis and Confederate general P.G.T. Beauregard stating that if Illinois could furnish two thousand men from her Knights of the Golden Circle lodges, the Confederate states would be fully able to succeed in winning independence from the Union. The letter recommended that Knights slip across the Federal lines in squads of two to four. Once in Dixie, they would be formed into full companies. Several

Knights expressed a willingness to go south, while others stated they could not leave their families.

The KGC members then affirmed their opposition to the Union draft by vowing to "resist it to the death" and to the federal tax, "even if necessary to raise an armed resistance." The meeting concluded with KGC members drilling and then practicing military tactics for an hour.

The *Tribune* article also provided information from the informant regarding secret codes used by the KGC. For example, if a member wanted to learn whether another man was a member, he "draws the forefinger of his left hand twice slowly across the upper lip." If he indeed was also a KGC member, the other man drew "the second finger of his left hand from the nose under the left eye." While such amateur theatrics seem ridiculous to modern readers, the KGC's passion for secret codes demonstrated its determination to remain clandestine.

Other witnesses quoted in the article affirmed the virulent racism of the KGC, as well as its hatred of abolitionists. A resident of Williamson County, located in deep southern Illinois, recalled a speech given at a local barbecue in which a KGC member argued that the South was justified in taking up arms against the federal government and that "the abolitionists were more to blame than the South and that they had brought on the war." The same witness heard W.J. Allen, an Illinois member of Congress, make a public address in which he claimed that the Lincoln administration "had commenced aright, but now they had commenced a war to free niggers."

Semple was not the only prominent southwestern Illinois politician who belonged to the KGC. Dr. Thomas Hope of Alton was also a member. Born in Virginia in 1812, Hope journeyed to Illinois and eventually settled in Alton in 1835 to establish a medical practice. Although a Whig, Hope detested abolitionists and bitterly opposed Elijah Lovejoy. During the Mexican-American War, Hope served as surgeon of the 2nd Regiment of Illinois Volunteers and saved the life of a young soldier named William Morrison, who would serve as colonel in the 49th Illinois Volunteers during the Civil War and was later elected to Congress from southwestern Illinois. Hope's competence as a physician and surgeon made him a popular figure in Alton, and he served as the city's mayor from 1851 to 1853.

When the Whig Party collapsed in the 1850s, Hope became a Democrat and aligned himself with the extreme proslavery wing of the party. The Democrats in the late 1850s were divided between supporters of President James Buchanan, who was characterized by his critics as a "doughface"—a northern Democrat who openly sympathized with the

South and slavery—and supporters of Stephen Douglas. The Illinois senator advocated "popular sovereignty," which maintained that residents of a state or territory should decide for themselves whether they wanted slavery within their borders. Hope unsuccessfully ran for Congress in 1858 as a Buchanan Democrat and heckled Douglas during his Alton debate with Republican senatorial candidate Abraham Lincoln.

As previously noted, the Democratic Party split asunder in 1860. Northern Democrats nominated Douglas for the presidency, while proslavery southern Democrats rallied behind Vice President John Breckinridge, who was supported by Buchanan. Hope ran for governor of Illinois as a pro-Breckinridge Democrat but lost the race to Richard Yates, a former Whig who ran as a Republican.

Hope loathed Lincoln and was outraged by his election to the presidency. When the Civil War broke out, according to an old *Telegraph* account, Hope "took the side of his native state and was strongly southern in his sympathies, which he was outspoken in expressing." Hope was particularly outspoken in 1862, when the Union army sought to rent a building he owned in downtown Alton for the purpose of drilling soldiers. The former mayor not only refused to rent his Third Street building but also condemned the Union war effort. "I want nothing to do with those whose hands are dripping with the blood of my friends in the South," he was quoted as telling a recruiting officer. Such bluntness brought charges of disloyalty to the Union, and Hope was interned in Alton's military prison, which I wrote about in *Abolitionism and the Civil War in Southwestern Illinois.*

Hope found the idleness of prison life intolerable and pleaded with his captors to put him to work. He was assigned to the prison hospital where, according to one account, Hope "did excellent service." Alton's former mayor was soon released from prison through the intercession of two Shurtleff College graduates: his wife, Penelope Pope Hope, and her brother, General John Pope. After a hearing in St. Louis, he was paroled on the condition that he must be more circumspect in his remarks regarding the Union and its campaign to suppress the rebellion. Hope observed this proviso and managed to avoid further incarceration.

Alton's townspeople forgave Hope's disloyalty, and he resumed his medical career. The Hope name was untarnished enough for Alexander Hope, his son, to be elected mayor of Alton in 1875. Thomas Hope died in 1885.

The *Tribune* article brought the KGC much unwanted publicity and, by revealing its secret codes, seriously compromised its ability to function covertly. According to Stephen Z. Starr, the organization's lack of effective central leadership also hampered its ability to disrupt the Union's attempt to put down the rebellion. Phineas C. Wright of St. Louis founded the Order of American Knights (OAK) in 1863, which absorbed the KGC and then embarked on an ambitious recruiting campaign in the Old Northwest and border states. One year later, the OAK claimed a membership of 300,000 to 500,000. Even if its actual strength was only a fraction of that number, as Starr observed, the OAK was powerful enough to disrupt or even sabotage the Union's war effort.

Congressman Clement Vallandigham, an Ohio Democrat and the most prominent Northerner who advocated an immediate conclusion of hostilities with the South, agreed to serve as supreme commander of the OAK on February 22, 1864. At the same time, the organization formally changed its name to the Sons of Liberty. The OAK leadership thought that adopting the name of a celebrated Revolutionary War band of Patriots would lend their group a greater degree of respectability. Another reason might have been that a society whose members referred to themselves as knights appeared curiously anachronistic in a modern republic. I. Winslow Ayer, in his *The Great North-Western Conspiracy in All Its Startling Details*, listed both Semple and Hope as members of the Sons of Liberty.

Vallandigham, whose wife was the daughter of a Maryland planter, was untroubled by the morality of the peculiar institution. He detested the abolitionists and two years earlier had delivered in Ohio a speech titled "Deliverance from Abolition Despotism." If the Sons of Liberty captured control of the Democratic Party and defeated the Republicans at the polls, he reasoned, the federal government would negotiate an immediate end to the war, even if it meant an independent South. Vallandigham thought that the Northwest might be better off joining the Confederate States of America than remaining in the Union when hostilities ceased. Alexander Stephens, vice-president of the Confederate States of America, had expressed a similar hope in 1861 when he wrote that "all the great states of the North West shall gravitate this way." Opponents of slavery in states such as Illinois would have been given the choice of repudiating their abolitionism or migrating to what remained of the United States.

The Sons of Liberty reached its nadir in 1864 when it attempted to foment an armed rebellion in Illinois. Thomas Henry Hines, a Confederate POW who had escaped from the Ohio State Penitentiary, made his way to Richmond, the capital of the Confederacy, and presented a plan that he believed would ensure the defeat of the Union. He asked authorization to recruit escaped Confederate POWs who were living in Canada and combine them with armed members of the Sons of Liberty to create a Confederate army behind Union lines. This army would then attack POW camps in Illinois, Indiana and Ohio to free their prisoners, which numbered in the tens of thousands. Copperheads in the Northwest would rise up against the federal government while this army of Confederate POWs moved south, cutting telegraph lines, pulling up railroad tracks and destroying every federal installation in its path. After entering Confederate territory, these marauders would unite with Rebel units in the field.

The Confederate government not only approved Hines's plan but also augmented it by authorizing Jacob Thompson of Mississippi, who had served as James Buchanan's secretary of the interior and was a close friend of Vallandigham, to go to Canada and coordinate Copperhead activity in Northern states. Thompson received $900,000 in greenbacks to finance this operation. He would pay a heavy price for abandoning his home for this Canadian adventure. In his *McKendree Pigskin* memoir of the 117th Illinois Infantry, Moore recalled, "After a fruitless campaign down to Oxford, Mississippi, where we burned old Jake Thompson's residence, while he was in Canada scheming to burn Chicago, we returned to Memphis to wash up and secure supplies."

Hines and the leadership of the Sons of Liberty agreed to launch this rebellion in Chicago on July 4, 1864, which marked the opening of the Democratic National Convention. Armed members of the Sons of Liberty from downstate Illinois would come to Chicago under the pretext of providing security for the convention and liberate the eight thousand Confederate POWs at nearby Camp Douglas. This combined Sons of Liberty/POW strike force would then move on to assault other prisons—including the one at Alton.

The uprising's date was postponed several times but was finally set for August 29. Hines and his band of Confederate agents in Chicago stood ready to launch their attack but lacked one thing: men willing to risk their lives in a military operation. Captain John B. Castleman, Hines's second in command, later recalled that the downstate Sons of Liberty who journeyed to the Windy City were "appalled" at the prospect of endangering their lives by participating in an armed assault on Camp Douglas. The exasperated Rebel conspirators were disgusted by the cowardice of the Sons of Liberty and blamed them for the mission's failure. Hines then made plans for assault on Camp Douglas that was scheduled for November 8—election day. The plot was betrayed, however, and a number of Chicago's Copperheads were arrested on charges of treason.

While the Northwest conspiracy was stillborn, there can be no doubt regarding the deadly earnestness of Hines and his associates, such as Charles Walsh, who served as brigadier general of the Sons of Liberty in Cook County. Authorities raided Walsh's house, which was located only a few hundred yards from Camp Douglas, and found 142 double-barrel shotguns, 349 revolvers and copious ammunition. Some have suggested that Walsh merely intended to smuggle the firearms to the Confederacy, but this theory is decisively refuted by the fact that every gun was not only loaded but also capped. These weapons were clearly intended for the Sons of Liberty to use in an insurrection.

Those members of the Knights of the Golden Circle in Jersey County who had proclaimed their support for the Confederacy back in 1862—much like all downstate Copperheads—were terrified when finally given an opportunity to engage in a military operation against Union forces. Drilling in gaily-colored uniforms on a prairie at night was one thing, but risking injury or death in combat with Union soldiers was quite something else. Defeated by the cowardice of its own members, the Sons of Liberty no longer posed a serious threat to the Union.

During the post–Civil War era, it became increasingly difficult to substantiate that the Knights of the Golden Circle or its succeeding organizations had even existed. Many of the official records were destroyed by upper-echelon members who feared arrest, while the rank and file insisted that they knew nothing and refused to talk. Some of these men were obviously embarrassed to admit their former disloyalty to the Union, while others were still intimidated by the flamboyant oaths they had taken that bound them to perpetual silence—as well as threats of death by torture for any member who revealed the secrets of these organizations.

A 2018 article on the Word Histories website states that an Illinois Copperhead made a lasting contribution to American English. According to I. Winslow Ayer in *The Great North-Western Conspiracy*, Chicago judge Buckner Stith Morris boasted that the thousands of Confederate prisoners at Camp Douglas, when liberated, would "send abolitionists to hell in a hand basket." This is the earliest recorded use of the phrase in the United States according to Word Histories.

Although long forgotten by southwestern Illinois residents, the Knights of the Golden Circle/Sons of Liberty were thrust back into the spotlight when the May 25, 1939 edition of the *Alton Evening Telegraph* contained a brief article about H.W. Miller, a resident of Rosedale in Jersey County. Miller razed an old log house and dug into the ground beneath it, where he found two earthen jugs. One jug contained a large number of gold and silver coins. Some of the coins dated back as far as 1787. "A number of the gold pieces are of octagon shape and bear the California mint mark," the newspaper reported.

The contents of the other jug were even more intriguing considering the fact that it was buried in the Union state of Illinois, as the jug contained several thousand dollars of Confederate currency. The bills were in denominations of $100, $500 and $1,000 for a total of about $5,000. It is not unreasonable to assume that Miller had discovered the treasury of southwestern Illinois's branch of the Knights of the Golden Circle/Sons of Liberty. The money had been earmarked to finance a rebellion in the Prairie State. Stillwell was well acquainted with his fellow Jersey County residents. He probably knew the men who had buried that money.

The Greene County Fairgrounds, located about a half mile from Carrollton, served as the "Camp of Instruction" for the regiment in which Stillwell enlisted. He and his brothers-in-arms marched out of Camp Carrollton early in the morning on February 27, 1862. The regiment reached Jerseyville, the seat of Jersey County, that evening and found "the sidewalks were thronged with country people," who sought to catch a final look at "their boy, brother, husband, or father."

Stillwell saw his parents, and it cheered his heart to see his mother "with a proud and happy smile on her face" upon seeing him for the first time in uniform. The troops, estimated by Stillwell to be "between 800 and 900 strong," were quartered in various Jerseyville buildings that night. The young man and his parents made their farewells in the local Baptist church. Stillwell's mother gave him some home-cooked food to take on journey, including "a big, fat hen full of stuffing."

Stillwell and the other recruits were supposed to march into Alton, but the residents of Jerseyville "turned out in force with their farm wagons, and insisted on hauling us to Alton." This caravan passed by "a popular and celebrated school for girls, called the 'Monticello Female Seminary.'" Stillwell estimated that at least one hundred Monticello students—with red, white and blue ribbons in their hair—stood by the side of the road and "waved white handkerchiefs and little flags at us, and looked their sweetest." He and the other men "stood up in the wagons, and swung our caps, and just whooped and hurrahed as long as those girls were in sight." The young recruits "always treasured this incident as a bright, precious link in the chain of memory."

Stillwell had earlier remarked that slavery was the cause of the Civil War. He and the other men had no way of knowing that Monticello College owed its very existence to slavery. Even the students of Monticello, as well as their parents, had no idea that this college had been founded as a restitution for having participated in the slave trade.

Benjamin Godfrey easily qualifies as one of the most enigmatic figures in American history. Entire segments of his life remain shrouded in mystery. Even Godfrey's date of birth is disputed, with some sources listing it as May 5, 1794, while others have it as December 4, 1794. All sources agree, however, that his birthplace was the Cape Cod village of Chatham, Massachusetts. His formal education was extremely limited, and he went to sea with his stepfather at age nine. Godfrey served in the U.S. Navy during the War of 1812 and was discharged in 1815. He moved to Baltimore and married Harriet Cooper in 1817.

Benjamin Godfrey founded Monticello Female Seminary in what is now the village of Godfrey. *Public domain image.*

Godfrey became captain of the brig *Emilie* in 1819 and transported slaves from Baltimore, which was the foremost slave-trading city in the Upper South, to New Orleans, the leading slave-trading city in the Lower South. In 1823, Godfrey voyaged from Baltimore to New Orleans and then sailed to Campeche, now the site of Galveston, Texas, and then on to Brazos Santiago, which was located near present-day South Padre Island, Texas. Campeche was the headquarters of Jean Lafitte, the notorious pirate who plundered Spanish ships carrying slaves and then sold the human cargo in New Orleans. Popular lore has long linked Godfrey with Lafitte in various nefarious enterprises, but there is no hard historical evidence to corroborate their association. As I noted in *Murder and Mayhem in Southwestern Illinois*, unfounded rumors claim that Lafitte is buried in Alton.

After surviving a shipwreck at Brazos Santiago in 1823 or 1824, Godfrey and his family settled in Matamoros, Mexico, a prominent smuggling port, although sources disagree regarding his activities at this time. He left Mexico in 1830 and arrived in Alton in 1832.

Sometime before he reached southwestern Illinois, this slave trader underwent a life-altering experience. One account claims that, while en route to New Orleans, Godfrey read a passage in the works of Emanuel Swedenborg, the theologian and mystic, that compelled him to change his values. Another source states that Godfrey struck a bargain with God during a near-fatal illness in which he promised that, in return for his recovery, he

would give half of his possessions to the Almighty. This second account, which was published in a Chicago newspaper in 1894, concluded that Godfrey's founding of Monticello Female Seminary represented "God's portion" of the former sea captain's wealth and thus fulfilled his promise.

While the true reason for such a profound change of heart may never be known, it is certain that the Benjamin Godfrey who arrived in Alton in 1832 bore no moral resemblance to the man who had trafficked in shackled human beings. It is also certain that Godfrey felt deeply ashamed of his role in the slave trade. When queried about his past, he simply replied that it would make a novel and then fell silent.

Godfrey chose to move to southwestern Illinois after a New Orleans meeting with Alton resident Winthrop Gilman, who persuaded the former sea captain to become his partner in a freight-forwarding business. In just three years, their firm was the most successful business in Illinois. Godfrey and Gilman soon extended their commercial enterprises to include banking, railroads and real estate.

But Godfrey wanted more than mere wealth. He wanted to better this fledgling community in which he and his family lived. Alton during this period justly deserved its reputation as a rough and rowdy river town, where liquor flowed freely in any number of taverns. Public inebriation was common, and fighting was both a participant and spectator sport. Determined to improve local morals, Godfrey spent thousands of dollars to purchase and

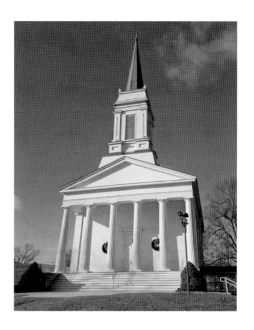

Opposite: Benjamin Godfrey's mansion is located just down the road from Monticello College, which is now Lewis and Clark Community College. The native limestone walls of Godfrey's residence are eighteen inches thick. *Photo by author.*

Right: Commissioned by Monticello Female Seminary founder Benjamin Godfrey, the Benjamin Godfrey Memorial Chapel was completed in 1854 in the New England Greek Revival style. It is located on the campus of Lewis and Clark Community College. *Photo by author.*

distribute Bibles, support the efforts of Protestant ministers and promote the temperance movement. But none of this satisfied his desire to make amends for engaging in the slave trade.

Godfrey claimed that the idea of founding a school for women occurred to him when he heard one of his children, who was just learning to talk, repeat a phrase his wife had just uttered. This simple incident served to drive home for Godfrey the unique influence that mothers have on their children. It also impressed him with the profound effect that educated women could exert on society as a whole. He decided to found a college where women could receive a quality education. Harriet Godfrey enthusiastically endorsed the idea, and Godfrey resolved to realize this goal.

It was a bold ambition for the time and location. Many American families, particularly those living in frontier communities, regarded education for women a waste of time and money. Women, it was thought, did not require a knowledge of mathematics, history and philosophy to prepare them for good marriages. Godfrey remained undeterred by such criticism but decided to designate his school a seminary rather than a college. "Seminary" conveyed the impression that the school was a distinctly religious enterprise in which students would be educated to become proper young ladies. Godfrey's subterfuge was not entirely successful, however. Area residents who gathered to watch the seminary's construction ridiculed it as "Godfrey's Folly."

Above: The grave of Benjamin Godfrey in Godfrey Cemetery identifies him as a veteran of the War of 1812. *Photo by author.*

Right: English artist William Granville Hastings cast this statue of Lincoln, which is located in Bunker Hill, Illinois. *Photo by author.*

Godfrey died in 1862 and took his secret with him to the grave. His involvement with the slave trade wasn't discovered until the twentieth century.

Monticello College formally opened in 1838 and thrived until the 1960s, when two-year colleges for women fell out of vogue. It closed in 1971 but was reopened as Lewis and Clark Community College. The village of Godfrey, Illinois, in which the author lives, is named for Benjamin Godfrey.

The Monticello ladies who cheered Stillwell and his fellow soldiers that day represented a greatly reduced student body. All the southern belles departed Monticello at the start of the Civil War and returned to their Dixie homes.

Stillwell and the others arrived at Alton around sundown and were taken aboard the *City of Alton*, a prominent local steamboat that readers of *Abolitionism and the Civil War in Southwestern Illinois* will recall had played a role in keeping St. Louis arms out of Rebel hands the previous year. There was no food for the men, so the officers went into Alton and used their own money to buy "a barrel of oyster crackers, called in those days 'butter crackers,' and our drink was river water." Upon arriving in St. Louis, the men marched to Benton Barracks, "which were clear out of town and beyond the suburbs." Benton Barracks, established in 1861, was located at the present site of St. Louis Fairgrounds Park. "While at Benton Barracks we were given our regimental number—Sixty-first—and thenceforth the regiment was known and designated as the Sixty-first Illinois Infantry." Stillwell and the other men were issued their weapons: Austrian-made muskets, which he praised as "a wicked shooter." They used these muskets until June 1863, when Stillwell and his comrades turned them in for American-made Springfield muskets.

Stillwell and his fellow soldiers left Benton Barracks on March 25, 1862, marched to St. Louis and boarded the *Empress*, a steamboat. "The city was enveloped in that pall of coal smoke for which St. Louis is celebrated," he recalled. "It hung heavy and low and set us all to coughing." The *Empress* took the 61st to Cairo, Illinois. The Ohio River had flooded that strategically important town located at the very tip of the Prairie State. Stillwell recalled that "the streets and the grounds generally were just a foul, stagnant swamp." Upon leaving Cairo by steamboat, Stillwell's deployment began in earnest. He participated in the Battle of Shiloh, the Siege of Corinth and other major engagements.

Stillwell welcomed his furloughs but wrote that "it seemed as if the citizens thought they must do everything in their power to show us how much they appreciated us. So there was something going on nearly all the time: parties, oyster suppers, and gatherings of all sorts." He appreciated this opportunity to spend time with his family, but there were constant interruptions "by the neighbors…who wanted to see and talk to 'Leander.'" Stillwell also wrote of a picnic in 1864 for all the local men who were home on furlough that featured a speech by a Jerseyville lawyer "in which he refreshed our recollections as to our brave deeds and patriotic services in battle, and in camp and field generally, which was undoubtedly very fine."

He and his comrades-in-arms rendezvoused at Springfield, Illinois, when this furlough ended and were transported by railroad to St. Louis, where they "were quartered in the Hickory Street Barracks, in the city." Stillwell recalled St. Louisans at that time feared an attack by Sterling Price, a former Missouri governor who now served as a Confederate general. "Judging from all the talk one heard," he wrote, "we were liable to hear the thunder of Price's cannon on the outskirts of the city any day."

This Jersey County resident's military service ended on September. 27, 1865. The following day, Stillwell boarded a train that took him from Springfield to Alton, where he hitched a ride with a teamster to Jerseyville.

From there he walked the distance to Otter Creek. Upon reaching the family farm, he found his father "cutting up and shocking corn."

The young veteran "doffed my uniform of first lieutenant, put on some of my father's old clothes, armed myself with a corn knife, and proceeded to wage war on the standing corn." The reader senses that Leander Stillwell much preferred this kind of combat. Stillwell, who later moved to Kansas, concluded this memoir by noting that "my humble career as a soldier in the 61st Illinois during the War for the Union is the record that I prize highest of all, and is the proudest recollection of my life." Stillwell died at age ninety on September 10, 1934, in Erie, Kansas.

William Scott

David Scott possesses two extraordinary mementos from his great-grandfather William H. Scott, who served in the Union army during the Civil War. One memento is his ancestor's .44-caliber Remington cap and ball revolver. The other is a journal in which Scott chronicled his wartime experiences. David Scott was good enough to send me a transcribed copy of this journal. Its entries bring the Civil War to life for modern readers.

Born in Lone Oak, Texas, on June 25, 1840, William Scott became an Illinoisan when his family moved to the Bond County community of Greenville just a few years later. He was mustered into Company D of the 22nd Illinois Infantry on June 25, 1861. Scott's Civil War journal begins with an entry dated May 1, 1862, when he was in Hardin County, Tennessee. It is uncertain why he waited so long to begin his journal.

May Day in times past was celebrated as the beginning of spring, and despite the war, Scott waxed poetic:

> *The sun never shined more brilliant than now. The birds are singing and the water in the little brooks ripples over the rocks and winds its way among the hills with all the beauty and sweetness for which Tennessee is remarkable. It seems strange that anyone could be unhappy on such a lovely day as this.*

But the natural beauty around him brought back painful memories of home:

> *And yet I feel a little sad as I think of home and the May parties, those happy groups whose voices are ringing in the groves and whose hands*

are eagerly plucking the first blossoms of spring; all joyous, happy and contented, while we poor soldiers already half dead from sickness, exposure and hard living are every moment expecting to hear the roll of the drum to call us into ranks for a march not knowing but what, ere the setting of the sun a Minié ball or a wicked piece of shell may assume intervention between us and worldly affairs and we be left lifeless upon the field of battle. Such is the consolation of a soldier.

Scott then noted that soldiers such as himself don't have the luxury of engaging in self-pity. Duty called:

I will stop my melancholy and get on my "traps" for the march. The enemy is before us and we are searching cautiously to subdue him and will in all probability meet him today in deadly combat.

According to Civil War reenactors, "traps" is short for trappings and refers to the gear carried by a soldier during a march. This included a wide leather belt for transporting boxes that held the paper cartridges of that era as well as percussion caps. A soldier's canteen and scabbarded bayonet hung from this belt. A soldier's gear would also include a haversack that held his plate, cup and rations.

He then closed this section of his memoir, which functions as a kind of preface, with some advice to civilians. Such an admonition could have been offered from anyone serving in the American armed forces during a war:

Then, enjoy yourselves fair ones at home. You know nothing of the trials of a soldier. For our country and you we will brave the dangers of battle; though you can never fully appreciate the hardships, dangers and disadvantages through which our duty daily leads us.

Early in the text, Scott provided a graphic description of a soldier's battlefield death. Interestingly enough, the soldier whose death he described with such pathos served in the Rebel army:

A wounded "Reb" was found lying in the brush some distance from the road. He was a mere boy about 14-years of age. His wound was a mortal one. Our boys carried him to the nearest house. He died on the way but lived long enough to tell us his name and residence. I went to the house to see the corpse. The face was pale, though calm and composed.

He was all gory with blood and an awful hole in his breast showed the entrance of the fatal bullet.

It was a touching scene to see one so young and seemingly innocent who an hour ago was buoyant with life and hope the victim of so sudden and horrid a death.

The fact that Union soldiers carried the dying boy to a house and took the trouble to learn his name and residence, presumably to inform his next of kin, demonstrates that the belligerents in this conflict were capable of showing compassion for the enemy when circumstances warranted it. The death of this boy, presumably far from his home and family, genuinely moved Scott.

An entry dated May 25, 1862, and written in Farmington, Mississippi, records Scott's dismay upon seeing his comrades engage in spendthrift behavior:

Everything is very quiet in our division today. Most of the troops have been paid off and the grove is full of gamblers. Sunday or Monday, it is all the same. From morning till night squads may be seen at church-a-luck poker or some other game, throwing away their money which might in some cases prevent a great deal of suffering if sent to their families at home.

The transcript of Scott's memoir indeed reads "church-a-luck poker or some other game." My guess is that he meant chuck-a-luck, which is a game played with dice.

Scott wrote on May 26, "Shouldn't be surprised if we saw the elephant tomorrow and if fighting begins it will present such a scene of carnage as eye never witnessed before." Most modern readers are probably unfamiliar with the nineteenth-century colloquial expression "saw the elephant." According to Dictionary.com, it means "experience more than one wants to, learn a hard lesson." First recorded in 1835, the expression conveyed "seeing all the sights one can see, including that rare beast, and returning home unimpressed or disappointed."

The troops were given whiskey rations in an attempt to ensure their good health:

For several days past a regular daily allowance of whiskey has been issued to the troops. This is considered necessary by our surgeons in order to counteract the influence of this unhealthy locality and to neutralize the effect upon the system of the impure water which we are compelled to use.

When potable water was lacking, whiskey served as a substitute. In a July 1 entry, Scott wrote that some soldiers "to supply the want of good water drained the dirty water from the mudholes in the road. We drew rations of whiskey this morning and perhaps never saw the time when it was more needed."

In his article "Forty Rod, Blue Ruin & Oh Be Joyful: Civil War Alcohol Abuse," David A. Norris wrote that "excessive drinking was a constant problem in both armies during the Civil War." He quoted Union general George McClellan's opinion that alcohol consumption "is by far the Greatest cause of the disorders which are examined by court martial." The surgeons mentioned by Scott weren't the only ones who possessed the authority to issue whiskey to troops during the Civil War. "A daily spirit ration for American soldiers had been abolished in 1832, but officers were permitted to issue special servings of whiskey to relieve fatigue and exposure," Norris observed. "Soldiers, naturally had countless sneaky ways to obtain whiskey."

Scott found a duel between artillery units a fascinating sight:

> *An artillery fight is a splendid scene when one is out of danger....I like to see a whole battery in line plugging away at the enemy all at once. I like to see the fire as it darts from the cannon's mouth and the monstrous curls of thick white smoke which rises so majestically in the air and the roar is so terrific.*

The term "friendly fire" was unknown during the Civil War, but Scott's journal entry for May 28, 1862, provides an example of this military mishap:

> *One poor fellow had his leg torn nearly off close up to his body by a cannon ball. Our sharp shooters were stationed in front of the battery and our guns fired over them but by some mismanagement a load or two of grape was thrown low and produced the sad results just mentioned.*

An entry for May 25, 1863, records an incident of friendly fire that borders on the absurd:

> *A member of the 27th Illinois Reg was severely and it supposed fatally wounded in the head this evening by the carelessness of our Brigade butcher. The butcher was engaged in killing a beef when having fired his piece the bullet missed its aim and struck in the head the poor man who was so unfortunate as to be standing exactly in range when the gun fired.*

June 29, 1862, fell on a Sunday, a fact reflected in Scott's journal entry:

This is another glorious and pleasant Sabbath morning. Oh how I would like to go to Union Grove to church today. I would like to see that hallowed spot once more and the happy faces of those who meet there to worship and whom I have not seen for more than a year. It is really a joy to me now to think of the place. I can almost imagine myself there and only wish that it was reality instead of imagination. But alas! Instead of going there as I used to do I must buckle on this miserable weighty box of powder and lead and gather my rifle and go on guard.

There currently is no city, village or township named Union Grove in Bond County. However, Union Grove Cemetery is located in the unincorporated community of Ayres.

Scott's entry for August 24, 1862, while in Franklin County, Alabama, contains a Civil War colloquialism. "We ascended a hill at the opposite base of which in a little valley were the supposed 'seceshers.'" This term is short for secessionists, those who supported secession from the Union. It applied to Confederate military personnel as well as Southern civilians. Scott painted an unflattering portrait of Confederate troops in his entry for New Year's Day 1863. He gives his location as Murfreesboro Battlefield, which is located in Tennessee. "I will not forget how they looked. They were dressed in dirty gray clothes and went sneaking along as if bent on the commission of some vile cowardly deed, while their appearance indicated the very personification of guilt and crime."

The entry for June 13, 1863, consists of a single sentence that reads, "Thirteen persons were baptized in Stone River today by Chaplain Raymond." Although he doesn't note it, Scott was surely aware of the irony of baptisms occurring in the body of water he called "Stone River," which is more accurately designated as Stones River or Stone's River. The Battle of Stones River raged from December 31, 1862, to January 3, 1863, when the Union's Army of the Cumberland under the command of General William S. Rosecrans clashed with Confederate general Braxton Bragg's Army of Tennessee. It was a Union victory but at a terrible cost for the North—12,906 casualties out of a force of 43,400.

In an earlier journal entry, Scott recalled Rosecrans reviewing his troops:

We were drawn up in a kind of half square and when all was ready General Rosecrans made his appearance and rode slowly along the line. He viewed the troops closely: nothing seemed to escape his observation. If there was a man who had no haversack or canteen he was sure to notice it and stop to inquire into the matter….He shook hands with the principal officers and sometimes stopped to talk with a Captain [to] inquire as to the health of the men and occasionally talk to the men in the ranks…getting off some witty remark.

Rosecrans "was accompanied by Maj. Gen. [Alexander McDowell] McCook, Gen. [Philip] Sheridan and Gen. [James] Garfield." Running as a Republican, Garfield was elected president in 1880. He was sworn into office on March 4, 1881, but shot by a deranged office-seeker on July 2. He clung to life until September 19.

Like most Civil War soldiers, Scott was compelled to forage for food. On Independence Day 1864, he wrote that his company as well as a company of the 27th Illinois were assigned to forage duty:

We went some three miles from camp to the rear with some half dozen wagons, found corn and fodder in the barn of an old planter sufficient to load a part of our wagons. We also found our way to the orchard and a fine garden where we appropriated whatever we could find that suited our tastes. Apples and potatoes disappeared in our haversacks with wonderful rapidity and peas, beans, beets, onions, currants and fine English grapes vanished before us like dew in the morning sun.

Scott and the other soldiers had no desire to condemn the planter and his family to starvation, however. He makes a point of noting that they "left corn enough for the use of the planter" before moving on to another farm for additional food. At this location, Scott and the others were delighted to find "a jug of whiskey which the old farmer had hid in the weeds."

A storm came up while the soldiers were still foraging. While Scott was standing guard in a stable, lightning struck his musket "from the barrel to the breech, then darted off upon me." He didn't immediately realize what had happened and thought that his body had been struck by a Minié ball or "a charge of grape shot had been thrown into my body." Assuming that the foragers had been discovered by Rebel soldiers, "I found myself anxiously peering through the crevices of the log wall in the direction which the shock had been received, looking for the supposed enemy."

Eagleville today is a small town of fewer than one thousand residents in the heart of Tennessee. Scott recalled it as "a small but neat village" that lacked "churches and other public buildings." However, he saw "two or three stores, a grocery or two and an Odd Fellows Lodge," which he noted "is always found in the villages of Tennessee and is (as I suppose) considered one of the indispensables." More properly known as the Independent Order of Odd Fellows (IOOF), this organization is a fraternal lodge that began in England. Although the precise year it was founded remains uncertain, the IOOF was in existence in the eighteenth century. The nineteenth century saw this fraternal order established in the United States. While not regarded as "indispensable," Odd Fellow lodges could be found across the United States in small towns as well as large cities. The IOOF is still very much still in existence. Odd Fellows proudly note that Ulysses S. Grant was a member of their order.

Scott and his fellow troops quickly discovered that Eagleville was no Union bastion:

> *When the Cavalry first entered the town a soldier went into the yard of one of the wealthiest men of the town whereupon the lady of the house having as I suppose a particular dislike to Yankees met him with a club in her hand and ordered him out. The soldier who had probably survived the dangers of half a dozen battles and not liking the idea of being repulsed by a woman refused to obey and the consequence was he received a blow from the cudgel of Mrs. Secesh. Enraged by such treatment the soldier raised his stalwart arm and struck her to the earth. Her daughter then came out and flourishing a pistol threatened to shoot the soldier: but she probably reflected that discretion is the greater part of valor at any rate she did not shoot. The Mother was confined to her bed on account of the stroke she received at the hands of the soldier when we left the town but it was thought she would recover in a day or two.*

"Discretion is the greater part of valor" is a slightly mangled line from Shakespeare's *Henry IV*, Part I. Prince Hal finds Falstaff lying on the battlefield and assumes that he was killed in combat. When Hal departs, Falstaff rises and states, "The better part of valor is discretion; in the which better part, I have saved my own life." Scott assumed that the angry daughter decided not to shoot the Yankee who had struck her mother because she suddenly realized that she would in turn be shot by his fellow soldiers. The fact that Scott alluded to this line demonstrates that he possessed some familiarity with literature.

Another journal entry has Scott referring to East Tennessee, which was a Union bastion in a Rebel state, as "the "Switzerland of America." That mountainous region of the Volunteer State was indeed known even in Scott's era as the Switzerland of America, although it's uncertain precisely when that designation came into vogue. Aaron Astor, a member of the history faculty at Maryville College, wrote a column for the *New York Times* in 2011 about that region's response to secession. He titled it "East Tennessee: The Switzerland of America."

While in Chattanooga, Scott described a poignant scene:

> *In the midst of a graveyard or rebel soldiers I noticed one "headboard" larger and more ornamental in shape and lettering than the rest. It was the grave of an Irish rebel soldier. The following inscription had been carved in the board by one of his fellows:*

> *"He sacrificed his life for his adopted country."*

Under which was the inscription by some good humored discriminating Yankee:

> *"And has gone to hell where all rebels go."*

That young Irishman's grave was something of an anomaly. Few Irish immigrants settled in the southern states. In his book *The Good Country: A History of the American Midwest, 1800–1900,* Jon K. Lauck wrote that Irish and German immigrants were reluctant to put down roots in the South because of its reputation for backwardness, especially illiteracy. Professor David Gleason, who studied the Irish in the Confederacy, arrived at the conclusion that 20,000 Irishmen fought for the South. Many sources state that approximately 150,000 Irishmen served in the Union army during the Civil War. An article posted on the website Irish in the American Civil War, however, contends that such a figure underestimates the number of Irishmen who fought in the Civil War. The article's author suggested that the figure should be in excess of 200,000. The Irish were indeed well represented in the Union army, as well as in our nation's navy. Richard D. Dunphy, an Irish immigrant, served as a coal heaver on the flagship of Admiral David Farragut and lost both arms during the Battle of Mobile Bay in 1864. For his heroism, Dunphy received the Medal of Honor.

The majority of residents living in eastern Tennessee had strongly opposed their state's secession and remained loyal to the Union. When Scott's unit entered Bradley County, "we saw some nice country and a great many Union people. The stars and stripes were floating from almost every house and men, women and children flocked to the roadside to see us." The fact that these Unionists gave such a warm welcome to the Yankee troops, however, didn't spare them the indignity of being robbed:

> *Notwithstanding we were in a Union settlement there was a great deal of foraging done. Those unprincipled scoundrels (and there are always some among every large body of men) could not, or rather would not, restrain their long cultivated propensity for stealing although among their friends. They killed chickens, geese and hogs and took bacon from the houses under the very eyes of the owners who pleaded in vain for them to leave that, they alone depended upon for subsistence. Such conduct might have been excusable if prompted by necessity but we had drawn plenty of rations and there was therefore no good excuse.*

This unprincipled foraging in a Unionist settlement was not without consequences, however. The very next day, an unnamed colonel unloaded on these troops:

> *He told them they had been robbing their own friends; that many of those whose property had been taken were officers and soldiers in our army. He concluded with an emphatic declaration that the next man caught committing depredations upon the property of citizens should be shot if he could get anyone to do it; if not he would do it himself.*

As an antique firearms enthusiast, I was intrigued by the Remington revolver that Scott brought home from the war and wondered why and how he acquired it. As a private, Scott's primary weapon would have been his musket. I asked David Scott in an e-mail how his ancestor had obtained what is now a treasured family heirloom. He replied that he didn't know. If I had just been a bit more patient, I would have found the answer to my question in the memoir.

The incidents recorded by Scott can sometimes be confusing to place in time since he doesn't always give a complete date. The entry that tells us why he acquired the Remington is simply dated "Saturday, 26th":

> *Lee Phillips and myself concluded to go out in the country today on a splurge and accordingly procured a pass and a couple of revolvers to defend ourselves against any guerrillas or hostile persons whom we might chance to*

William Scott brought home his Remington revolver from the Civil War. It's now a family heirloom. *David Scott.*

meet, went up town, stepped aboard the outgoing train with as much show of authority as though we had be Major Generals (although in fact we had no right there)…rode to Mouse Creek Station…went to the Hotel, had a most splendid dinner; got a pint bottle full of brain destroyer for which we paid two dollars and proceeded on our journey.

This entry also mentioned Scott's encounters with women he calls "factory girls," a term that in days past was applied to all young women who worked in factories. They assured him

that most of the citizens in that locality were secesh though there were some Union people there, who had brothers, husbands, fathers, and sons in the Federal ranks.…The rebel ladies told us of their husbands and lovers in the Southern army and how they prayed for their success and wished for the destruction on the "Blue coats" as they called us. One said she used to admire blue but of late she had seen so much of it and had become so disgusted with those who wore it that she wished she might never see anything blue again.

Scott was delighted upon meeting a woman who proudly declared herself to be a "Union girl" and confided to his journal that "I had discovered an oasis in the desert of treason." He "felt like imprinting a Union kiss upon her lips but alas!…the heart's best sympathy—decorum—forbade."

As he had on May Day 1862, Scott praised the natural beauty he saw around him on May 1, 1864, while in Cleveland, Tennessee. Although a drenching rain had fallen the previous night, the morning of May Day "dawned bright and beautiful. The sun rose majestically in the clear sky shedding its golden hues in glorious tints over the partially mantled forest." It cheered Scott's heart to watch sunbeams "playing beautifully upon the lingering drops of water which hung from the tips of the tender half-grown leaves. It was just the morning to inspire a soldier with vigor and healthful hilarity."

Scott wasn't alone in his enjoyment of this May Day:

> *All seemed to enjoy themselves uncommonly well today. Many tender epistles were* [written] *to friends and loved ones in the far away North and thus the evening closed upon a happy day in camp. Some of the boys went to church while others remained in their quarters. But alas! It makes me sad to think that it will in all probability be the last meeting for many who have helped to swell during the past week those large and attentive audiences under the salutary labors of the gentlemanly agents of the Christian Commission.*

Founded in November 1861 at a convention called by the Young Men's Christian Association (YMCA), the U.S. Christian Commission (USCC) provided Union forces with Protestant chaplains who conducted religious services, as Scott notes in his journal. The USCC also worked with the U.S. Sanitary Commission in providing medical services. According to an article on the Reenactors of the Civil War website, the five thousand volunteers, called "delegates," carried no weapons "but were sustained by sharing the love of Christ with soldiers and sailors." During the war, the USCC "distributed more than $6 million worth of goods and supplies in hospitals, camps, prisons and battlefields." That's the equivalent of about $96 million in today's money.

A journal entry for May 4, 1864, stated that he "camped once more upon the soil of Georgia within six miles of Ringgold," which is a town in northern Georgia. "This country here is rough but rather hilly than mountainous. The people in this section are known as Sand-hillious." The author searched in vain for any further information regarding the term "Sand-hillious."

Scott's journal entry for May 7 again demonstrated that this young soldier, who was so far from home and loved ones, could revel in the natural beauty he saw around him:

> *The weather was warm and pleasant and the air fragrant with the perfume of May flowers. The forest looked grand. The little valleys and hillsides were thickly studded with wild honeysuckle whose blossoms reveling in the sunlight lit the verdant woods with a gorgeous glow. The tall pines waved to and fro in the breeze, birds were alive to the season and as they flitted around, warbling their* [mating] *songs so cheerily I began to think that*

William Scott with his family long after the Civil War.
David Scott.

army life is not so dreary after all. Happiness was visible on every face and beauty perched on every branch. It was just such a scene I imagine as poets and painters delight to dwell upon.

Scott concluded his memoir by noting his authorship:

Written by

> *William H. Scott, H.P.R.R. (High Private Rear Rank),*
> *Company D, 22nd Illinois Voluntary Infantry,*
> *3rd Brigade, 2nd Division, 4th Army Corps,*
> *Department of the Cumberland,*
> *Military Division of the Mississippi,*
> *Army of the United States of America.*

Ringgold, Walker County, Georgia, May 8th, 1864.

Scott was mustered out of the army on July 7, 1864. In an e-mail, David Scott informed me that his great-grandfather married Josephine Wightman in Greenville on May 5, 1870. "They returned to Lone Oak, TX shortly after and my grandfather, Charles Scott, was born there in 1882," David Scott stated. "The family returned to Greenville in 1885 and then move[d] to Wood River, IL in 1910. My grandfather, Charles Scott, married Hilda Kohler in 1915 in Alton, they lived in Upper Alton on College Ave and later on Judson Ave." David Scott noted that he was "unable to locate any information on the date William Scott died or where he was living at the time."

William R. Eddington

The Madison County Historical Society has posted on its website several wartime accounts written by long-ago area residents. William R. Eddington, who was born in the Macoupin County town of Woodburn in 1844, wrote his Civil War memoir, titled *My Civil War Memoirs and Other Reminiscences*, shortly before his death in 1936. His sharp memory and candid words bring the Civil War to life for modern readers.

Eddington's upbringing was marred by alcoholism and domestic violence. "My father was a drunkard," he wrote, who often sent him "to a little town two miles distance to buy whiskey for him. In those days every grocery store and street corner sold whiskey. The price was 20 to 25 cents per gallon." Eddington's father sometimes "would not draw a sober breath for two weeks at a time."

Violence was a regular occurrence in the Eddington household:

> *I have seen him take a gun and try to shoot my Mother and shoot the candle light out. I have seen him many times take a butcher knife and take after my Mother and drive her out doors, where she had to hide out in the brush all night to keep away from him. I have seen this many times.*

Eddington's father died on January 4, 1855, at the age of forty-three. "He drank himself to death," Eddington wrote. His mother died in 1896 at eighty-two. Eddington had eight siblings, all of whom were deceased when he wrote his memoir.

His education was limited. There was no free public school where he lived until he was fourteen. Private schools, which parents financed by paying tuition, were held in a succession of residences. Despite his spotty schooling, Eddington at age nineteen "taught a six months school in the new school house."

When the war broke out in 1861, Eddington's widowed mother refused to allow her underage son to enlist. One year later, however, she relented. This young man and "four of the neighborhood boys" journeyed to Gillespie to enlist in the Union army. They were sent to Camp Butler for training. Later, these young men "were put on cars on the Chicago and Alton R.R. and started for Alton." Upon arriving, they were placed on a train destined for Terre Haute, Indiana. Pioneers had been calling Illinois the "prairie state" since at least 1842. Eddington's memoir reveals why. He wrote "as we rolled along the great prairies of Illinois for miles and miles, there was not a house to be seen—nothing but a great ocean of wild prairie grass waving in the wind higher than a man's head."

Eddington, who served in Company A of the 97th Illinois Volunteer Infantry, was blunt about the hardships he endured. While in Kentucky, he wrote about marching through a snowstorm. He and the other men pitched their blankets on the ground that night and, "too weary to eat," tried to get some rest. The next morning, they discovered that their "blankets were frozen solid to the ground."

Upon taking Fort Hindman at Arkansas Post in January 1863, Eddington and the other Union troops discovered "a lot of new Enfield Rifles which had been smuggled to them [the Confederates] from England." Eddington and many others eagerly exchanged their muskets for these English-made weapons, which they regarded as superior in quality. Were Eddington and his fellow Yanks correct in that assumption? In an article titled "Springfield vs. Enfield" posted on the NRA Museum website, Philip Schreier painstaking examined both weapons and noted that "there was much greater interchangeability between different Springfields than there was between Enfields." On the other hand, "The Enfield certainly had a more sophisticated sighting mechanism, though practically speaking, the guns were rarely fired at distances much greater than 200 yards." So which was the superior weapon? "Firing tests of both guns show similar accuracy and reliability, so that's pretty much a wash."

They took about five thousand Confederate prisoners who were placed on boats and sent "to Alton, Illinois, where they were put in the Old State Penitentiary and kept there as prisoners of war for about two years." The wounded of both armies were placed on "hospital boats" and then taken to hospitals. Eddington grimly noted, "Many of them had to have their legs or arms cut off....Such are the horrors of war."

Eddington's description of the Arkansas Post battlefield is brutally frank. He saw a man lying on the ground and thought that he was asleep since he appeared unharmed. Upon rolling this man onto his side, however, "I saw that the whole back of his head was shot out." While the man's face was untouched, his head "was hollowed just like a gourd." Eddington also wrote of seeing a dead man who was lying on his back, "but his feet were standing up in front of him in a long legged pair of boots." This soldier's legs had been blown off just above his boots.

Eddington's account of the fall of Vicksburg to the Union army on July 4, 1863, gives readers insight into the hardship and deprivation endured by Civil War soldiers. Upon surrendering, he noted, the Rebel prisoners "were allowed to come out and mingle all together with the Union forces." The Rebels were ravenously hungry: "Many of them had not had a bite to eat for forty-eight hours. We opened our haversacks and gave them everything we had—even to the last hardtack. They even had eaten their last mule and did not have one left. They had eaten even all the rats they could catch."

Eddington conceded, however, that he and his fellow Union soldiers were a sorry lot as well:

> We felt pretty dirty and lousy too, as we had not had a clean stick of anything to put on for more than six weeks and we were covered with graybacks [slang for lice], as we had not had any chance to clean up for the past two and a half months, not even to pick them off. Sometimes were unable to get water enough to wash our faces for two weeks at a time, and other times some of our trenches did not have outlets and when it rained we had to take our caps and bail the water out with them so we could stay in them. We were a miserable looking set. I doubt if our own mothers would have recognized us if they saw us.

Hunger stalked these men. When rations ran low, Eddington recalled troops ripping the bark from elm trees and chewing it while they marched. While in Alabama, Eddington and his officer asked a woman seated by the door of a plantation house if they could have something to eat. The woman not only refused them food but also added that she hoped "God would strike every Yankee dead before they got off her place." However, a "colored boy" who lived on the plantation brought the invaders some bread, ham and eggs.

While awaiting the order to launch the "big charge" against Fort Blakeley in Alabama, "we knew that many of us would never see the light of another day," he recalled. The pain from that moment haunted him for the rest of his life, even as he wrote his memoir. "The tears are running down over my cheeks so fast they blind my eyes and I have to stop and wipe them away."

Eddington returned to Brighton after his discharge. The ground he tilled as a farmer surely contrasted sharply with the corpse-strewn battlefields of the Civil War.

Most Union veterans associated the Republican Party with loyalty to the nation and victory in the Civil War. Eddington concluded his memoir by stating, "In politics I am a Republican. I have voted seventeen times for president and always for a Republican." The Democratic Party for Eddington and his fellow veterans was the party of treason and slavery. "I believe in freedom and liberty and this is something we get very little of under a Democratic administration." Writing seventy-one years after the Civil War's conclusion, Eddington was still bitter over what he saw as the treachery of the Democratic Party. "The war of their party['s] rebellion took the lives of 640,000 of the boys of the North and it can never be known how many Mothers died from worry and broken hearts against that party's great rebellion against liberty and freedom."

Eddington was mistaken, of course, when he claimed that 640,000 "boys of the North" died during the Civil War. His 640,000 figure is close to the total number of Civil War casualties on both sides: 624,511. That number, from the e-history site of Ohio State University, becomes even more horrifying in light of the fact that it represents about 2 percent of the American population at the time. The OSU site notes that 224,580 Union military personnel died of disease, while 164,000 Confederates perished from disease.

For some reason, Eddington felt compelled to note that his life had been austere to a degree that seems astonishing to modern readers:

> *I never drank a glass of any kind of liquor in my life. I have never used tobacco in any shape, form, or fashion. I have never played a game of cards.…I never played a game of dice or chuckaluck* [sic]. *Never played a game of baseball, football or basketball. Never bet or gambled in any way. Never was inside a theater or hospital.…I never go to prize fights or horse races. I never danced.*

Eddington then shared the values that had guided him through life:

> *My policy is to love and serve God to the very best of my ability. To love my neighbor as I do myself and to do unto others as I would like then to do unto me. This is the only road there is to true happiness in the world and the life that is to come hereafter.*

Eddington closed his memoir with an uncharacteristic boast: "I think this is the longest article ever written by a ninety-two Civil War veteran. It has approximately 22,100 words." He then signed off with his name, outfit and address:

Lieutenant W.R. Eddington
Co. A 97th Reg. Ill. Vol. Inf.
R.F.D. 1, Box 51
Brighton, Illinois

Although a civilian for sixty-six years, he still identified himself as Lieutenant W.R. Eddington. His military service had forever defined him.

PRISONERS OF WAR

Andrew Rodgers

Born in Howard County, Missouri, in 1827, Andrew Fuller Rodgers became a resident of Upper Alton in 1833 when his family moved to the village. He was one of twelve children born to Reverend Ebenezer and Prunella Rodgers. The Rodgers family lived on a forty-acre farm. According to the *Alton Evening Telegraph*, Ebenezer Rodgers "was one of the founders of Shurtleff College and one of its early trustees." Andrew Rodgers "was one of the early students of Shurtleff College."

Young Rodgers "became a clerk in a St. Louis hardware establishment" in 1844 but returned to Upper Alton just before the United States went to war with Mexico. He joined the army and served as a private in Company E of the 2nd Illinois Volunteers. "Brave and possessing the fire and determination so necessary, he was the ideal soldier," the *Alton Evening Telegraph* stated. "He gave distinguished service with his regiment in a number of engagements, the chief of which was Buena Vista."

The Battle of Buena Vista was fought February 22–23, 1847. General (and future president) Zachary Taylor commanded the American forces, while Santa Anna led a much larger Mexican army. Santa Anna withdrew his army from the battleground due to lack of food for his men. The Mexican army, however, captured American flags and cannons, which were placed on display in Mexico for decades following the war.

Illinois resident and Whig congressman John J. Hardin served as a colonel in the 1st Illinois Infantry during the war with Mexico. He was killed during the Battle of Buena Vista. The village of Hardin, which is the seat of southwestern Illinois's Calhoun County, is named in honor of John J. Hardin.

Rodgers then participated in the California Gold Rush and, while still mining, was appointed to the position of deputy sheriff by Sacramento sheriff Benjamin McCulloch, who had also fought in the Mexican-American War. Ironically, McCulloch would later serve as a brigadier general in the Confederate army.

In a long article commemorating Rodgers's life, the *Alton Evening Telegraph* reported that he not only survived a shipwreck but also managed to save a fellow passenger. He had returned home "for a visit" and was on his way back to California "when his vessel was wrecked in the Pacific in 1853 with the loss of 250 passengers. Col. Rodgers with a few other survivors was cast on Marguretta Island." He saved the life of "a girl passenger." The survivors were picked up by a whaling vessel that brought them to San Francisco. "Fifty years later," the article reads, "he learned that the girl he saved was living in St. Louis, the mother of a clergyman in the Episcopal church." Since Upper Alton is less than thirty miles from the Gateway City, we may assume that Rodgers and that long-ago girl celebrated a joyous reunion.

Rodgers returned to Alton when his father died in 1854 and worked the family farm and its sawmill. He married in 1860. And then our nation plunged into the Civil War. According to the *Alton Evening Telegraph*:

> *In 1862 he entered service as captain of Company B of the Eightieth Illinois Infantry, and when the troops were mustered in on August 25 of the same year, he was appointed lieutenant colonel of the regiment.*
>
> *His service in the Civil War was ardous* [sic]*, eventful and of a distinguished order. He was carried from the field of battle at Perryville, Ky. wounded.*

Fought on October 8, 1862, the Battle of Perryville was the largest Civil War battle fought in Kentucky. The Union army, under the command of Major General Don Carlos Buell, carried the day but at a tremendous cost. The Blue and the Gray suffered a combined total of 7,621 casualties. Defeated Confederate general Braxton Bragg observed that "for the time engaged it was the severest and most desperately contested engagement within my knowledge."

Rodgers, the Illinois 80th and four other Union units participated in Streight's Raid in northern Alabama from April 19 to May 3, 1863. Union troops under the command of Colonel Abel Streight were assigned the task of destroying portions of the Western Atlantic Railroad, which ran supplies to Confederate forces in Tennessee.

Streight's men were hampered by lack of supplies. Exhausted, they stopped to rest at Cedar Bluff, Alabama. According to historian Keith Hebert, "To make matters worse, during a recent skirmish the soldiers learned that the bulk of their ammunition was rendered useless due to its exposure to water." Streight had about 1,700 men but surrendered to General Nathan Bedford Forrest, who commanded a force of only 500 Confederate troops. "Forrest's artillery repeatedly rode in circles in and out of Streight's view along a neighboring ridge," Hebert wrote. "On May 3, 1863, Streight surrendered, convinced he had been captured by a numerically superior foe."

Rodgers and the other Union officers were taken to Richmond, Virginia, where they were incarcerated in Libby Prison. Hebert wrote, "In 1864, Streight and 107 other prisoners escaped through an intricate system of tunnels." While a celebrated escape from Libby indeed occurred in 1864, Rodgers was not one of its participants. Accounts in the *Alton Evening Telegraph* and *Portrait and Biographical Record of Madison County, Illinois* agree that Rodgers remained in Libby for twelve months before being sent to a prison in Macon, Georgia. The prisoners were then transported to Charleston, South Carolina. The newspaper states that Rodgers "and other officers were placed in a cell directly in line with the enemy's fire, and in this perilous position remained for six weeks, until released by exchange [of prisoners]."

By "enemy's fire," the reporter probably meant fire from Union artillery. The city of Charleston had been under siege by Union forces since July 10, 1863, and endured heavy bombardment. By placing Rodgers and his fellow prisoners "directly in line" with Union artillery fire, their Confederate captors used these men as human shields. Charleston didn't surrender until February 18, 1865.

Rodgers was commissioned a full colonel while still a prisoner. Upon his return to Illinois, Governor Richard Yates and General William Rosecrans asked Rodgers to recruit men for a new regiment: the Illinois 144th Infantry. The *Portrait and Biographical* record notes that "this he did, raising two hundred men, for which the Government was to give him two hundred drafted men. This was not done and he resigned November 25, 1864, having paid out of his own pocket $2,000 in recruiting these men."

Rodgers was a Mason. Before leaving Alton, some friends gave him a sword that bore a Masonic symbol as well as his name. This sword was taken from Rodgers when he was taken prisoner. Fifty years later, according to the *Alton Evening Telegraph*:

> *Col. Rodgers was informed by the adjunct general of Illinois that a man in Texas was seeking an officer by name of A.F. Rodgers. The sword was returned to the Alton officer by the brother of the man who led the Southern troops which captured Col. Rodger's [sic] force. The sword had been used in a Texas Masonic lodge as the tyler sword.*

Rodgers returned to farming and entered politics, serving one term as a state representative. While other southwestern Illinois veterans gave their allegiance to the Republican Party, Rodgers ran as a Democrat. He was later elected mayor of Upper Alton. A 1912 work titled *Alton, Illinois: A Graphic Sketch of a Picturesque and Busy City* includes a photograph of Rodgers. The caption identifies him thusly: "In 1912, One of Alton's Most Highly Esteemed Citizens." The village Upper Alton had been annexed by the City of Alton the previous year, so the old soldier had become a citizen of Alton. The caption misidentifies his unit as the 8th (rather than the 80th) Volunteers. Rodgers died on January 22, 1922, at age ninety-four.

JOHN T. KING

Robert Kellogg's 1865 book *Life and Death in Rebel Prisons* contains a chilling account of some Union prisoners of war who were taken to Camp Sumter, which is better known to us as Andersonville prison. As he and his fellow POWs entered, one man stated, "Before us were forms that had once been active and erect—stalwart men, now mere walking skeletons, covered with filth and vermin." These horrified new arrivals wondered aloud, "Can this be hell?" In a sense, they were right.

Opened in February 1864 and eventually covering 26.5 acres near the town of Andersonville, Georgia, this Confederate prison camp housed as many as forty-five thousand Union inmates. At least thirteen thousand men died during their incarceration. Food was alternately scarce or nonexistent, while the small creek meant to provide water for the inmates was choked with filth. Disease was rampant, especially scurvy and dysentery. At least

Entered according to Act of Congress, in 1865, by A J. RIDDLE, in office of Dist. Court of U. S. for South'n Dist. of N.Y.

ANDERSONVILLE PRISON, GEORGIA.

South-east View, taken from the Stockade.

Thirty three Thousand Prisoners in Bastile.

Photographed by A. J. Riddle,   August 17th, 1864.

Camp Sumter, better known as Andersonville, proved to be a living hell for its Union prisoners of war. *Library of Congress.*

two Union soldiers from southwestern Illinois—Charles Wentworth of Edwardsville and William W. Jones of Hillsboro—died in Andersonville. John T. King of Upper Alton, Illinois, who served in Company F of the 115th Illinois Infantry, survived that living hell and even left a firsthand account of his experiences. I challenge anyone who thinks history is boring to read his narrative, which the *Century Magazine* published in 1891.

Captured in 1863 while foraging for supplies in Tennessee, King and the other Union prisoners were promptly robbed of their personal possessions by the Rebels, who even ordered their captives to exchange clothing with them. The Rebels "forced us at the point of a bayonet to repair the railroad" at Chickamauga, "which had been burned during the battle."

The Union prisoners eventually were transported by rail to Richmond, Virginia, and incarcerated in Libby prison, which had once been a tobacco warehouse. The air inside was stifling, so King seated himself by an open window "and was drawn in by a fellow prisoner, or I would have been shot by an outside guard." King and the others were later moved to another tobacco storehouse, where their rations were "two to four ounces of beef and six to eight ounces of good wheat bread." To supplement such meager fare, the prisoners forged greenbacks that they used to purchase additional food. King recalled that "it was the only time when I was in the Confederacy that I had a full meal."

While being moved by railroad to Danville, Virginia, King and three other prisoners escaped by jumping from the train. "After five days and nights of almost superhuman effort and suffering," however, they were recaptured and taken to Danville for further incarceration.

An escape attempt at Danville brought four hundred Union prisoners the punishment of confinement in a room that was built to hold no more than two hundred. A few men who could no longer bear such hell forced open a window and leaped to the ground. They were immediately riddled with buckshot. Those not killed were returned to the confinement room, where King and the others "dug out some of the shot as best we could." Another prisoner was shot by an inside guard when he held a can of soup through the window "to pour off some of the bugs."

King and his fellow prisoners arrived at Andersonville on May 20, 1864. His account noted that of the four men who had escaped from that train en route to Danville, only he survived incarceration in Andersonville. "Prisoners kept pouring in," he noted, "and thousands who had no vestige of a blanket" burrowed holes in the ground for protection against the elements. Minuscule portions of meat and poorly baked bread formed the inadequate provisions. Later, "yams, rice or peas were issued in lieu of meat, and meal or grits instead of bread."

Since the men were given no vessels to receive rations, they were forced to improvise. King recalled some men who removed their trousers, knotted up one leg and then received their portion of the food. Since the stream meant to provide water for Andersonville's

Henry Wirz served as commandant of the notorious Andersonville prison. *National Park Service, Andersonville National Historic Site.*

inmates was little more than an open sewer, he and a few other inmates used half canteens and even sticks to dig a twenty-foot well that yielded "only drops of water."

Disease and malnutrition ensured a high mortality rate at Andersonville. "Death came slowly," King recalled. "It seemed a gradual wearing out." Brutality by the prison guards also took its toll. King saw one man who had been mauled after guards set the prison hounds on him. "I could have fought off the dogs," the man told his fellow inmates, "but the men cocked their revolvers and made me come down from the tree, and then set on the dogs until they got tired."

The guards' brutality was emulated by some inmates, who began to prey on the weaker prisoners. "They snatched and ate the rations of the weaker ones and they grew stronger," King stated. "We called them 'raiders' and they grew in numbers and boldness until murder was added to theft and no one was safe." The other prisoners organized themselves into a squad called the regulators, and the two sides warred with each other. "The stockade was pandemonium those days," King noted. "Hundreds of half-naked men here, and hundreds there, surged to and fro, with sticks and fists for weapons."

The occupation of Atlanta by Sherman's Union forces on September 2, 1864, compelled the Confederacy to transfer Andersonville inmates to other prisons. King was evacuated to a prison in Florence, South Carolina, where conditions were also horrendous. "The rations were uncooked and more scant," he recalled. The commandant "used to hang up by the thumbs men who had escaped and been retaken," King noted. "I heard their shrieks in the long nights."

King was one of the prisoners freed by parole from this hell on December 7, 1864. Once safely aboard a Union ship that journeyed to Rebel-held Fort Sumter to take them home, some of the former prisoners cheered and literally danced with joy. Others, King said, "knelt in silent prayer, and tears cut furrows down grimy cheeks where they had long been strangers." A number of men began cursing the Confederacy for the hardships they had endured, as well as Lincoln and Grant for hampering the exchange of prisoners.

Somehow, King managed to accumulate small bag of grits during his most recent incarceration. He wrote:

> *I could not eat the grits but dared not let then go until I knew that we were surely free. I had starved so long that those broken kernels were very precious. I was constantly hoping to barter them for something that I could*

eat, or possibly for a dose of quinine or some peppers. But now a gang plank was run from some opening in the side of the transport. It was lined on each side by sailors who pushed us rapidly along the big vessel.

King and the other ex-POWs were ordered to strip off their filthy clothes, which were then unceremoniously chucked through a porthole. Their clothing was filthy, he recalled, and "were the remnants of what we had worn a year and half before in the Chattanooga campaign, remnants of what we had taken from the dead." Such rags, he noted, "had been held together by threads raveled by the stronger parts and held together by needles made from the splinters of Georgia pine." After being issued new clothing, each man was given a pound of wheat bread, a half pound of raw pork fat (described by King as "the sweetest morsel I ever tasted") and a pint of coffee. Now decently clothed and fed, King reported that "lost manhood began to return." In other words, these ex-POWs began to feel like human beings rather than animals who had to fight tooth and nail for their very survival.

Five of these liberated prisoners died before they reached Annapolis, where the men were again stripped and washed. "We were put to bed between white sheets," King noted. One can scarcely imagine the joy these men experienced while lying in clean, comfortable beds. For the first time in years, they were treated with kindness:

Women came to my cot with oysters fresh from the bay, with bread and butter, jellies and pickles, with shining glass and snow-white napkins, and when I had eaten they said, "Now you just rest and sleep, and dream of home." When I was able to read the card at the head of my cot, I found: "Phthisis pulmonalis, fever, general debility; diet treatment." I cannot remember the diet or the treatment, but I remember well the ministrations of those women; how they hovered around my cot, touching up my pillow, and how their cool hands rested on my hot forehead. I do not know whether they were army nurses, residents of Annapolis, or members of the Christian and Sanitary commissions. But the soldiers have never forgotten their ministrations, and give to women's loyalty and patriotism a "royal three times three."

A "royal three times three" is an archaic expression for the cheer we know as "Hip hip hooray."

Pneumonia prevented King from returning to active service, but he wasn't discharged from the army until the war ended. He moved to Colorado, where he married Ruth Dorsey and fathered two daughters. His obituary in the *Alton Evening Telegraph* noted that he engaged in farming, school teaching and business. When he relocated to Upper Alton, King opened a business on College Avenue and later "had charge of the local power house at Sixth and Piasa streets," which is an intersection in the city of Alton.

King took an active interest in maintaining the Oakwood Cemetery, now known as the Upper Alton Cemetery, and served as its director for a number of years. Many Civil War veterans are buried there, including Major Franklin Moore, with whom King was acquainted. Serving as cemetery director was King's way of honoring his old Union comrades. His obituary also noted that King was "gifted with a talent for public speaking and writing, and his pen was a busy one." His writings on the Civil War, the obituary noted, "had contributed much to the authentic facts of the struggle, as he had a good memory and was a close student of Civil War history."

In 1924, at age seventy-nine, King finally retired, turned over his Upper Alton business as well as the building that housed it to his granddaughter Marjorie Dietiker and went to Denver to make his home with his daughter. His wife had died in 1890. When King died in 1934—just ten days after reaching ninety—his body was returned to Upper Alton for interment at Oakwood Cemetery. John T. King joined the other Union veterans who rested in the cemetery that had been entrusted to his care for so many years.

JOSEPH WEEKS

Born in New York City on January 26, 1836, Joseph H. Weeks attended public schools in Brooklyn and became a carpenter. He journeyed to Illinois in 1857 and settled in Upper Alton in 1860. His father had fought for the United States during the War of 1812. When the Civil War broke out, Weeks followed his father's example and answered the call for volunteers by enlisting in Company F of the 32nd Illinois Infantry on September 1, 1861. He was mustered in as a sergeant at Camp Butler.

According to his obituary, "On January 31, 1862 his regiment was ordered to Cairo, Illinois, where it was one of the few comprising Grant's Army of the Tennessee. Two months later he was appointed color sergeant, having in the meantime been assigned to the first brigade, Fourth division, under General [Stephen] Hurlbut."

Being appointed color sergeant was no small honor. Soldiers who carried their unit's colors bore a crucial responsibility during the Civil War. Smokeless gunpowder wasn't invented until the 1880s, which meant that Civil War battlefields often came to resemble London during a particularly heavy fog. As Savannah Labee noted in the online article "For Duty, Honor and Family: Color Bearers in the Civil War," these flags "helped soldiers see where their units were located in the confusing, smoke-filled battlefield." In addition, flags served their units outside of combat. Color bearers "also set the pace for the march, making sure it as the proper length and cadence," Labee wrote. "The flags helped to establish a group identity and gave the men something to fight for, which explains why there are so many stories of drastic measures taken by soldiers to prevent their colors from being captured."

Irish-born Patrick Highland, a corporal in Company D of the 23rd Illinois Infantry, received the Medal of Honor for "conspicuous gallantry in the assault on Fort Gregg" at Petersburg, Virginia, on April 2, 1865. Capturing the enemy's colors also brought one acclaim. Simeon T. Josselyn, who served as a lieutenant in Company C of the 13th Illinois Infantry, also received the Medal of Honor. The citation reads: "While commanding his company, deployed as skirmishers, came upon a large body of the enemy, taking a number of them prisoner. Lt. Josselyn himself shot their color bearer, seized the colors and brought them back to his regiment."

That Rebel color bearer posed no threat to Josselyn. As Labee noted, "Color bearers didn't carry weapons, increasing their likeliness of being killed or wounded. If a color bearer happened to be shot down, a member of his guard would immediately pick up the colors in order to avoid the disgrace of losing one." Obviously, no other Confederate picked up the flag of the Rebel shot by Josselyn.

Joseph Weeks soon learned firsthand the danger associated with serving in the color guard, which his obituary succinctly summed up in a single sentence: "Then came the battle of Shiloh, in which of his Color Guard of seven men, six were either killed or wounded."

The horrors of war didn't deter Weeks from continuing to serve his country. "The weary months that followed are matters of history, and Mr. Weeks experienced no less hardships than the others. January 2, 1864 he re-enlisted at Nachez [sic], Mississippi, and in February came home on a brief veteran's furlough."

Unlike his fellow Upper Alton resident John T. King, Weeks was taciturn about his wartime experiences. However, he granted an interview to an unnamed *Alton Evening Telegraph* reporter in 1886. The reporter duly noted that "Captain Weeks of Upper Alton is a very modest man, and the article below was not volunteered by him, but was related to a *Telegraph* reporter after persistent urging by the latter, and protestations of reluctance on the part of the gallant Captain."

Weeks begins his story with the furlough that would later be mentioned in his obituary: "The boys of the old Thirty-Second Illinois Infantry will never forget the return to the front after their veteran furlough. Having feasted and enjoyed all that mothers, wives, and sisters could do for them, they were not in a good condition to make a 390-mile forced march over rough roads, on short rations." Weeks and his comrades-in-arms

> *left Cairo on May 10, 1864, on an expedition under command of General Frank Blair (composed of the veterans from the 4th and 5th Divisions of the 17th Army Corps), who had orders to hasten to the front and reinforce Sherman. They embarked on two gunboats and 12 transports, and arrived at Clifton on the Tennessee River on May 14. On May 16, they started on a march across the State of Alabama, by way of Huntsville and Decatur.*

Weeks recalled that the route took them over a mountainous region and cited Sand Mountain in particular. It was a dangerous journey:

> *Some places the roadway was out in the sides of the mountain overlooking a precipice, and so narrow that it was difficult for a team to pass. A sudden pitch or a rough jolt against one of the many boulders which lay in the roadway was sufficient to upset a wagon and send it down the mountainside. Several such accidents occurred, but no lives were lost.*

Mountainous terrain wasn't the only danger:

> *During a greater part of the route they were annoyed by Roddy's [sic] rebel cavalry. Having some 200 head of cattle and a large supply train, they had to be continually on the alert. Near Decatur, the Federal cavalry, under Colonel Long, had a brisk fight with Roddy's [sic] command, which resulted in favor of the Union soldiers, who captured forty prisoners. They joined Sherman's army at Ackworth, Georgia, about June 10.*

Confederate brigadier general Phillip Dale Roddey, who was mentioned in that March 30, 1864 edition of the *Montgomery (AL) Advertiser*, served as commander of the district of northern Alabama. In September 1864,

Roddey was tasked with protecting northern Alabama and given the nickname "Defender of North Alabama," according to Joshua Shiver of Auburn University. He formally surrendered to Federal troops on May 16, 1865, at Pond Springs, Alabama. Less than a year later, he was granted a full pardon by the administration of President Andrew Johnson.

The newspaper account continued:

> The 32nd found the Union army in line of battle within sight of Kennesaw Mountain. The Federal and Confederate forces were daily in conflict, and had been for many days, and there was scarcely a day that the 32nd was not under fire, from June 10 until early in September, a period of more than three months. After the fall of Atlanta, the 32nd was sent to guard a water tank. On October 3, Hood's army, having flanked Sherman, captured and destroyed the railroad between Big Shanty and Altoona, at which time Captain Weeks, while in command of Company F, and while in advance picket duty, was captured within a few yards of the rebel rifle pits.

John Bell Hood was a West Point graduate who rose to the rank of major general in the Confederate army. A daring and reckless commander, he lost a leg at Chickamauga. He launched four unsuccessful offenses seeking to break Sherman's Siege of Atlanta. He was defeated at the Battle of Nashville, December 15–16, 1864, by Union major general George H. Thomas, who had been one of his instructors at West Point.

Weeks owed his capture to a literal misstep:

> Briefly, the facts were these: Captain Weeks had taken five picked men of his company, and was feeling his way toward the enemy when a sudden charge was made by the rebels, and the scouting party retired, Captain Weeks being the last to retreat. In crossing a creek at the foot of a ravine, Captain Week's foot slipped and he fell, and on rising was confronted by a rebel officer's cocked revolver, so he had to submit to the exigencies of the occasion and yield as gracefully as possible.

Weeks told the reporter that the following morning, he and "300 other Federal prisoners of the 14th and 15th Illinois, and 4 of Company C of the 32nd Infantry, who were captured under somewhat similar circumstances," were marched under guard to Lost Mountain. Currently an unincorporated area in Cobb County, Georgia, the summit is so named for a Native American legend. These prisoners "were quartered for the night in a hog pen near

General Hood's headquarters" and fed "scanty rations of cornmeal and raw beef being issued, which were cooked without any cooking appliances in the embers of the campfires."

This forced march resumed the next morning and took the prisoners through the towns of West Point and Columbus. "While marching through Columbus," Weeks recalled, "the rebels seemed to take great delight in showing their Yankee prisoners to the admiring citizens, who manifested as much curiosity as if the Federals formed part of an itinerant menagerie of wild beasts." Accommodations were primitive. "The prisoners were first taken to the Columbus Cemetery, where they were on view during the day, and at night they were quartered in a stable yard, with only two blankets for every six prisoners, and the nights were already cold and disagreeable."

Upon arriving at Andersonville, Weeks and the other prisoners were placed in the Bull Pen, which he described as "a piece of swampy ground about thirty acres in extent, enclosed by three stockades." He saw thousands of Federal prisoners, "a large proportion of whom were sick with scurvy and diarrhea, and all were reduced to mere skeletons, and the average number of deaths among the captives was about 40 per diem, that is in the stockade and at the hospital." The Andersonville hospital "was such only in name, as it consisted solely of a shed with open sides. In fact, only a roof perched on poles. Men only went to this place as a dernier resort, the majority preferring to stand outside rather than to enter the medical post house, where their treatment was simply dreadful, no attention being paid to the sanitary state of the inmates."

His description of the prisoners' horrendous diet is much more detailed than King's account. The reporter wrote:

> *At the time of Captain Weeks' arrival at Andersonville, the rations for the prisoners were cooked outside the camp, and consisted of four inches square of cornbread, a spoonful of rice, and a spoonful of molasses with a few black beans occasionally. Subsequently, the prisoners claiming that even these scant rations were not honestly supplied them, the raw cornmeal and rice were issued in an uncooked state. The cornmeal was the only part of the ration regularly supplied, the rice and molasses being served out about once a week. About once in a month, a handful of salt was issued, but the quantity was not more than sufficient to cook one meal per man. About once in five or six weeks, a ration of one ounce of bacon was issued to each prisoner, but this was in such a state as to be unfit for human food. The water in which the prisoners' food had to be cooked passed through the rebel camp, and was used by the Confederates as a common sewer.*

If such inhumane treatment was intended to break the prisoners' spirits, it succeeded. Weeks told the reporter, "The prisoners, by this dreadful treatment, were reduced to a state of despair and cared for nothing." Like King, Weeks devoted part of his account to the prisoners' housing. "The first thought of the prisoners on entering the stockade was to find shelter. This consisted of holes in the ground dug out as best they could with half pieces of empty canteens and scraps of any old metal that could be got. The holes were covered with boughs of trees in some cases, and some were mere furrows in the side of a bank."

Prison personnel readily helped themselves to the inmates' clothing. "The men were literally in rags and tatters, and their condition was simply intolerable. Their clothings [*sic*], such as was in any ways comfortable, was taken from them, only enough being left to actually cover sufficient of their bodies to comply with the demands of ordinary decency."

In addition to stealing their clothing, the Rebels refused to allow local residents to supplement the prisoners' meager food rations. "At one time," the newspaper account stated, "during the imprisonment of Captain Weeks, a Southern lady, from motives of pure humanity, tried to supply the Yankee prisoners with sausage meat, prepared by herself, but she was stopped in her humane labor by the cowardly Major Birch, who vilified her in every way and finally used his drawn revolver, pointed at her head, before he could compel her to desist in her charitable undertaking."

Davis Duffey, park guide at Andersonville National Historic Site, responded to my inquiry regarding "the cowardly Major Birch." His e-mail stated, "After doing some research, I was not able to find any reference to the Major Birch incident. The only two Andersonville guards I were able to locate in our database were both privates and spelled their name Burch." The article concluded thus:

With regard to Major [sic] *Wirz, the notorious commander of Andersonville, Captain Weeks does not hold him personally responsible at all, but says he was simply the tool of the rebel Generals, some of whom are now in the United States Congress, and others representing this country abroad. This fact is Captain Weeks' reason for thus briefly allowing his prison record to appear in print. Otherwise, he would prefer to say nothing of what he went through while doing his part to sustain the honor of the American flag and the integrity of the Union.*

Born as Hartmann Heinrich Wirz in Switzerland 1822, Wirz held the rank of captain, not major, in the Confederate army. He was arrested at Andersonville on May 7, 1865, and tried for conspiracy and murder by a military tribunal in Washington, D.C., from August 23 to October 18. He was found guilty, condemned to death and hanged on November 10, 1865.

Wirz granted an interview to the *Evening Star*, a newspaper based in Washington, D.C., just before his execution. He told the reporter, "As far as I am concerned, I have no hope of reprieve" and conceded that he "had never denied the prisoners were mistreated." Wirz maintained "It was not my fault. If I am the last one to suffer death for the Southern Confederacy, I am satisfied." The condemned man stated, "I do not fear death." He then reaffirmed his innocence. "I never saw a man shot nor never [*sic*] shot one myself." Wirz also maintained that he "never hunted prisoners with the dogs."

The account of his execution that appeared in the *New York Times* corroborated Wirz's claim that he didn't fear death:

> *Nobody who saw him die to-day will think any the less of him. He disappointed all those who expected to see him quiver at the brink of death.*

The execution of Henry Wirz for war crimes. *Library of Congress.*

He met his fate, not with bravado, or defiance, but with a quiet, cheerful indifference. Smiles even played upon his countenance until the black coat shut out from his eyes the sunlight and the world forever.

Wirz's notoriety made souvenirs from his execution highly desirable, according to the *New York Times* reporter:

No sooner had the scaffold and the rope done its work, and become historically famous, than relic seekers began their work. Splinters from the scaffold were cut off like kindling wood, and a dozen feet of rope disappeared almost instantly. The interposition of the guard only saved the whole thing from being carried off in this manner.

Photos of Wirz's hanging show the scaffold surrounded by Union troops bearing muskets fitted with bayonets. Perhaps the "relic seekers" were soldiers.

Weeks was correct upon asserting that some former Rebels were now serving in Congress. No less than sixty-three ex-Confederates served in the U.S. Senate after the Civil War. The last former Rebel to serve in the senate was Charles Thomas, who held a Colorado seat from 1913 to 1921. Just a year before Weeks granted this interview, President Grover Cleveland appointed two former Confederates to his cabinet: Augustus Hill Garland as attorney general and Lucius Q.C. Lamar as secretary of the interior. Garland had served in both the Confederate House of Representatives and its Senate. Cleveland in 1888 nominated Lamar to the U.S. Supreme Court, and he was confirmed by the U.S. Senate.

Weeks surely wasn't the only Union veteran who was appalled by the success enjoyed by his former enemies. Still, the appointments were hardly surprising. Cleveland was the first Democrat elected to the presidency in post–Civil War America. The former Confederate states were now solidly Democratic, and their voters had overwhelmingly cast their ballots for Cleveland. Appointing Lamar and Garland was payment of a political debt.

Weeks spent seven months in Andersonville, according to his obituary. Upon release and "his return to the Union lines he was a mere skeleton, almost blind and with limbs crippled by scurvy." Weeks told the reporter that his hip bones literally projected through his skin. He suffered from poor health for the rest of his life. After months in a hospital, he rejoined his regiment in Washington, which "was ordered to Louisville, St. Louis and finally to Fort Leavenworth, where he received his commission as Captain, dated July 5, and on September 16, 1865, with his regiment, he was mustered out and returned to his home in Upper Alton."

This Union veteran married Martha L. Mills, the daughter of an Upper Alton minister, less than a month after his return to that village. They had one child before Martha's death in 1869. Weeks married Martha M. McGill in 1873, by whom he had six children. A Republican, Weeks served as Upper Alton's postmaster during the administrations of GOP presidents Rutherford Hayes and Benjamin Harrison, both of whom served as Union generals during the Civil War. He died on July 13, 1913. In the purple prose of that era, the obituary writer observed, "His last years have been full of physical distress and pain, but he has borne all with a wonderful patience and resignation. He has rounded out a life of devotion to his God, his family, and his country, and leaves a fragrant memory behind him."

George C. Uzzell

Biographical information regarding the Uzzell family is contradictory. George Uzzell's obituary stated that his death in Bethalto on October 20, 1907, at age seventy-four "removes one of the pioneer residents of Madison County. He had lived here for almost three quarters of a century, and his father came here almost a century ago, having removed to St. Jacob after the battle of New Orleans in January 1815, where he fought under Andy Jackson."

However, the unnamed author of an article titled "The Lone Confederate Grave in the Cemetery at Bethalto" who interviewed J.U. Uzzell, one of George Uzzell's sons, offered a different story.

A Huguenot family who fled to England to avoid persecution, the Uzzells immigrated to "the James river settlement in Virginia long before the American Revolution; thence, eventually westward to Illinois, and to Bond county." Bond County or Madison County? It is a matter of record that Mary Jane Bilyeu Uzzell, George's wife, was indeed born in Bond County, and the couple were married in that county in 1857.

Despite his family's southern roots, George C. Uzzell—often abbreviated in old accounts as G.C. Uzzell—sympathized with the North and became a supporter of the Republican Party. In the election of 1860, Lincoln carried Bond County. However, the author of "The Lone Confederate Grave in the Cemetery at Bethalto" wrote that "there was a strong element of Southern sympathizers" where Uzzell lived. Indeed, "in that particular precinct or voting district where the Uzzells lived there were but two votes cast for Abraham Lincoln. Of course, everyone knew who had cast these votes."

When the Civil War began, the Knights of the Golden Circle embarked on a campaign to cleanse Bond County of its Republicans. Uzzell and the other man who had voted for Lincoln began receiving threatening messages, replete with drawings of skull and crossbones. A short time later, that other man was shot dead under mysterious circumstances. According to the author of "Lone Confederate Grave":

> [I]t was told about the country that the man who was suspected of having done the shooting turned up as the owner of a very fine gray riding horse that had belonged to the wife of the man who was killed. As was only too often the case, the bitterness of the war divided families, and in this one instance it was a matter of comment that husband and wife were divided in sentiment, the wife being a strong sympathizer with the Confederacy and reputed, though of course no one could definitely say so, a member of the mysterious Knights of the Golden Circle. It was said by some that the woman herself had presented her fine horse to the man into whose possession it had passed.

Uzzell was also marked for murder. While working alone in the woods to fulfill a contract for supplying stave lumber, he heard the sound of crackling in the brush. Uzzell instantly sprang for his rifle, cocked its hammer and pointed the muzzle in the direction of the sound. In less than a heartbeat, Uzzell was staring at another man whose rifle was pointed at him. After a few moments of awkward silence, the man greeted Uzzell and said that he was hunting squirrels. Uzzell and the hunter exchanged a few mundane pleasantries and then parted company.

That evening, however, Uzzell's suspicion that the mysterious hunter had been seeking game other than squirrel was confirmed by a neighborhood woman who told him that his life was in danger. She had heard her husband and other Bond county men plotting to kill him. The woman begged Uzzell to leave the region for his own good—and to ensure that her husband's hands wouldn't be stained with the blood of an innocent man.

Uzzell decided to take the woman's advice. Lacking money and uncertain where to go to begin his life anew, Uzzell decided to enlist in the Union army and served as a sergeant in Company E of the 130th Illinois Infantry. While participating in Major General Nathaniel Banks's Red River Campaign in 1864, Uzzell was captured and sent to Camp Ford, a prisoner of war facility located near Tyler, Texas.

Covering eleven acres, Camp Ford was the largest Confederate prison west of the Mississippi and held more than 5,300 Union POWs. Unlike the living hells that were Libby and Andersonville, Camp Ford was one of the least lethal Civil War prisons, with a death rate of less than 7 percent. Prisoners were allowed to leave the camp under guard to tend a large vegetable garden, while an occasional butchered steer provided protein. A stream yielded adequate fresh water. Prisoners were required to build their own shelters, however, which were sometimes nothing more than brush arbors or burrows dug into hillsides. The camp administration allowed inmates to write letters to their families that were mailed postage-due. Captain William May, an inmate with a literary flair, managed to produce three issues of an underground camp newspaper called the *Old Flag*, which he literally hand-wrote. May smuggled copies from the camp by concealing them under his epaulets.

One day, while walking inside the stockade, Uzzell was hailed by the armed guard atop the wall. "Look out, Yank!" the guard shouted. "You're getting mighty close to the dead line." It was an ominous warning. The dead line was a marked boundary that a prisoner could be shot without warning if he crossed.

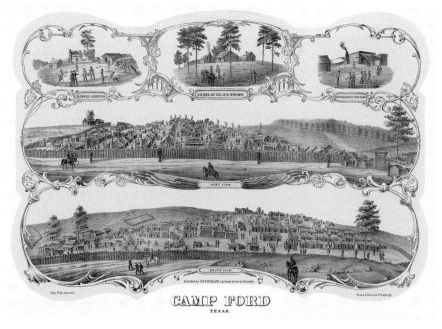

Camp Ford, where George Uzzell was incarcerated as a prisoner of war. *Public domain image.*

Uzzell looked up at the guard who had cautioned him. "What're you looking at, Yank?" the Confederate asked. "See anything green up here?"

"Nothing green," Uzzell replied, "but somehow or other there's something about your voice seems to take hold of me. And your features, too, they seem to be just dimly familiar, as if I see them in a dream."

The guard was amused by Uzzell's speculations and said, "I guess you never saw me before, in dream or any other way. But who do you imagine I look like?"

"Can't say that I imagine you look like anyone in particular," the prisoner said, "but way back yonder when I was a little bit of a shaver, so young that I really can't say I remember about it, I had a brother, who went away from home. He was older than I, and I just have a hazy sort of picture of his leaving and hearing the folks talk about him."

Uzzell turned to walk away. Suddenly, the guard called out, "Hold on, Yank; wait a minute? What was your brother's name, and where did your folks live?" When Uzzell replied that his brother's name was Leonard Uzzell and that his family lived in Bond County, Illinois, the guard said, "Well, I guess I'm that fellow. That's my name, and that's where my folks used to live."

Upon being relieved of guard duty, Leonard Uzzell immediately reported to the camp administration that he had a brother who was an inmate. George Uzzell was summoned to headquarters, and the two brothers—so long separated by years and miles—were finally able to greet each other. Although reunited, however, the Uzzell brothers were still divided by national allegiance. George Uzzell was shortly returned to the inmate population of Camp Ford.

Leonard Uzzell persuaded his superiors to offer George a chance for freedom. The inmate was brought to headquarters and told that he would be paroled if he swore allegiance to the Confederacy. Leonard Uzzell, who was present, told George that he would be sent to a plantation in Texas and could run the place until after the war. George, however, was a loyal Unionist and chose continued incarceration over freedom. Ironically, George's decision to remain at Camp Ford led to his brother leaving the site. The camp administration felt that it was unfair and inhumane to expect brother to guard brother, even if one of the brothers was a Yankee. Leonard Uzzell was transferred from Camp Ford.

The camp was finally closed on May 5, 1865—about six weeks after Lee's surrender at Appomattox. The 10th Illinois Cavalry celebrated Independence Day in 1865 by destroying Camp Ford, and today the site of the stockade is a community park.

EPILOGUE

Perhaps the fact that his life had been threatened by his neighbors in Bond County made Union army veteran George Uzzell reluctant to return to his prewar home. In any event, he chose to resume his civilian life in Madison County. He was soon joined by Leonard, who wanted to make his home with his Yankee brother rather than live in the defeated South.

The Civil War divided many American families, and it was not unusual for brothers to serve in rival armies. After the war, most of these brothers reconciled—few more successfully than the Uzzells, who became the best of friends. When Leonard died in 1871, he was buried at what is now the United Methodist Church Cemetery on West Corbin Street in Bethalto. George died in 1908. George's obituary in the *Alton Evening Telegraph* was titled "Man Dies After Sun Stroke" and stated that this proud Union veteran had been sun struck two months earlier "and laid in the hot sun for several hours before he was found. He never rallied from this illness, the end coming yesterday afternoon." Uzzell's wife died seven years later and was buried next to her husband in Bethalto's Methodist Cemetery.

Memorial Day, which earlier generations of southwestern Illinoisans typically called Decoration Day, was established by John A. Logan, a southern Illinoisan who served as a Union general during the Civil War. As national commander of the Grand Army of the Republic, an organization for Union veterans, Logan in 1868 issued General Order No. 11, which designated May 30 as a day for decorating the graves of Union soldiers.

This Parrott rifle monument commemorating the Union dead was placed at Alton's City Cemetery in 1890 by the Grand Army of the Republic. *Photo by author.*

Southwestern Illinois was particularly diligent in observing this tradition. According to the author of "Lone Confederate Grave":

The memories of the heroes of the war are kept alive by the beautiful annual custom of strewing flowers on the graves of the men who gave their lives that the nation might live.

In no place is this custom more faithfully and fervently observed than in Madison County, and the ceremony of decorating the little heaps of sod beneath which the brave men of the war "sleep the sleep that knows no waking" is a solemn and reverent one. There are a considerable number of these war heroes buried in the Bethalto cemetery, and year after year the graves of these men are given attention.

The grave of Leonard Uzzell, however, was never strewn with flowers. Decoration Day, after all, was founded to honor deceased Union troops—not the Rebels they had fought. The article mentions a particularly memorable Decoration Day when Leonard's grave received a generous offering of flowers, courtesy of a determined elderly woman who loudly expressed her displeasure that the cemetery's lone Confederate grave was ignored each May 30. Addressing herself to the throng who had gathered to decorate Union graves, the unnamed woman angrily proclaimed:

Maybe he [Leonard Uzzell] was a rebel, as we call 'em. He would have been a traitor if he had not been a rebel. We are all good Union folks, we on this side; but suppose we had been on the other side of the fence—wouldn't we have all been good Confederates?

The article concluded with this comment: "And never since then has any single soldier's grave been neglected on Memorial Day in that cemetery." While that might have been true in 1912, however, the practice of decorating Union graves was gradually discontinued as the Civil War became a fading memory. American casualties in World War I, World War II, Korea, Vietnam and more recent conflicts accounted for many newer graves to decorate on Memorial Day. Honoring the Union dead was no longer a priority.

The unusual saga of Leonard Uzzell, whose full name was John Leonard Uzzell, came to the attention of some local history enthusiasts in 2000, and they decided to honor the cemetery's lone Confederate. They replaced Uzzell's crumbling tombstone with a new grave marker that noted his service in the Confederate army. The dedication ceremony featured a performance of "Bonnie Blue Flag," a popular marching song of the Confederacy, by the Bethalto High School band. Members of the Sons of Confederate Veterans Major General Bushrod Johnson Camp 1718, which is indeed named after the Bushrod Johnson who was formerly buried at Miles Station Cemetery, also attended the event.

Reverend Howard White, pastor of Bethalto's United Methodist Church, delivered the invocation and benediction. He asked that God wash away the pain of the Civil War as well as its symbols, such as the Confederate flag. While it could be justifiably displayed at a ceremony such as one to dedicate a Confederate veteran's new tombstone, White declared, the Confederate flag was often used in the contemporary United States as a symbol of hate.

I couldn't agree more. Displays of the Confederate flag, the symbol of a short-lived nation that enshrined slavery as its cornerstone, should be limited to museums and historical reenactments. The flag of southwestern Illinois is the American flag, which proudly flies daily outside the Dunphy Building in downtown Alton. The Stars and Stripes commemorates this building's use as an Underground Railroad station during the pre–Civil War era. It also honors the courageous soldiers of southwestern Illinois who risked—and sometimes gave—their lives to save the Union and destroy slavery.

BIBLIOGRAPHY

Alabama Judicial System. "Daniel Coleman." https://judicial.alabama.gov/Docs/ library/Bios/DanielColeman.pdf.

American Battlefield Trust. "Ten Facts: Perryville." https://www.battlefields.org/ learn/articles/10-facts-perryville.

American History Central. "Bushrod Rust Johnson." https://www. americanhistorycentral.com/entries/bushrod-rust-johnson.

Ayer, I. Windslow. *The Great North-Western Conspiracy in All Its Startling Details.* Authorama Public Domain Books. www.authorama.com/north-western-conspiracy-1.html.

"'Blue' Colonel and 'Gray' General, Tale Traders, Rest in Miles Cemetery." *Alton (IL) Evening Telegraph*, May 31 1932.

Cashon, John P. "Paducah—Gateway to the Confederacy." Essential Civil War Curriculum. https://www.essentialcivilwarcurriculum.com/paducah-gateway-to-the-confederacy.html.

Centennial McKendree College with St. Clair County History. Lebanon, IL: McKendree College, 1928.

David, Duffey E. E-mail to the author, February 7, 2022.

"Death of Gen. Bushrod Johnson." *Alton (IL) Telegraph*, September 16, 1880.

DeLand, T.A., and Smith A. Davis. *Northern Alabama: Historical and Biographical Sketches*. Chicago: Donohue and Henneberry, 1888.

Eddy, Thomas Mears. *The Patriotism of Illinois*. Chicago: Clarke and Company, 1865.

"Execution of Wirz." *Evening Star* (Washington, D.C.), November 10, 1865.

"Execution of Wirz." *New York Times*, November 10, 1865.

"Funeral of Col. J.R. Miles." *Alton (IL) Evening Telegraph*, April 3, 1903.

Gerling, Edwin G. *117th Illinois Infantry Volunteers, 1862–1865*. N.p.: privately printed, 1992.

Hageman, Mark C. "Espionage in the Civil War. Signal Corps Association, 1860–1865," Civil War Signals. http://www.civilwarsignals.org/pages/spy/spy.html.

Hamlin, Griffith A. *Monticello: The Biography of a College*. Fulton, MO: Ovid Bell Press, 1976.

Harrison, Lowell H. "Slavery in Kentucky: A Civil War Casualty." *Kentucky Review* 5, no. 1 (Fall 1983).

Hebert, Keith S. "Streight's Raid." Encyclopedia of Alabama. http://www.encyclopediaofalabama.org/article/h-1380.

"Hero of Two Wars Dies at Home Here." *Alton Evening Telegraph*, January 20, 1922.

Hillig, Terry. "'McKendree Regiment' in Civil War Remembered." *St. Louis Post-Dispatch*, May 23, 2008.

History of Macoupin County, Illinois. Philadelphia, PA: Brink, McDonough & Company, 1879.

History of Madison County, Illinois. Illustrated with Biographical Sketches of Many Prominent Men and Pioneers. Edwardsville, IL: W.R. Brink and Company, 1882.

Hoffman, Judy. *God's Portion: Godfrey, Illinois, 1817–1865*. Nashville, TN: Cold Tree Press, 2005.

Hosmer, Charles B., and Paul O. Williams. *Elsah: A Historic Guidebook*. Elsah, IL: Historic Elsah Foundation, 1979.

"Joseph H. Weeks, Civil War Veteran, Prisoner at Andersonville." Obituary. *Alton (IL) Evening Telegraph*, July 13, 1906.

Kulp, Jim. "Ceremony Honors Civil War Soldier with Headstone." *Telegraph* (Alton, IL), October 2, 2000.

Lauck, Jon K. *The Good Country: A History of the American Midwest, 1800–1900*. Norman: University of Oklahoma Press, 2022.

"Lincoln Monument." *Alton (IL) Evening Telegraph*, August 25, 1904.

"The Lone Confederate Grave in the Cemetery at Bethalto." *Edwardsville Intelligencer*. Madison County centennial edition, 1912.

"Major Moore's Funeral." *Alton (IL) Evening Telegraph*, July 14, 1905.

"Major Moore's Next Campfire." *Alton (IL) Evening Telegraph*, August 4, 1904.

"Major Moore Surrenders in Last Battle." *Alton (IL) Evening Telegraph*, July 12, 1905.

"Major Moore's Will Probated Today." *Alton (IL) Evening Telegraph*, September 5, 1905.

"Man Dies After Sun Stroke." *Alton (IL) Evening Telegraph*, October 21, 1907.

Meszaros, Nina. "Body of Confederate General to Be Moved from Brighton Grave to Tennessee Home." August 5, 1975.

———. "South's Final Drumroll for General Bushrod." *Alton (IL) Telegraph*, October 1, 1977.

Missouri Digital Record. Soldiers' Records, War of 1812–World War I. https://s1.sos.mo.gov/records/archives/archivesdb/soldiers/Results.aspx.

Mitchell, Barbara J. *O' Fairest Monticello*. Hallstead, PA: Freedom Acres Press, 2000.

Morrison, Marion. *A History of the Ninth Regiment, Illinois Volunteer Infantry*. Monmouth, IL: John S. Clark, 1864.

Nager, Eric. "The Impact of the Civil War on Elsah." *Elsah History*, no. 58 (1990).

National Park Service. "Captain Henry Wirz." https://www.nps.gov/ande/learn/historyculture/captain_henry_wirz.htm.

Norton, W.T., ed. *Centennial History of Madison County, Illinois and Its People, 1812–1912*. Chicago: Lewis Publishing Company, 1912.

O'Neil, Tim. "Eads Built Civil War Gunboats Here." *St. Louis Post-Dispatch*, September 4, 2011.

Palmer, George Thomas. *A Conscientious Turncoat: The Story of John M. Palmer*. New Haven, CT: Yale University Press, 1941.

Palmer, John M. *Personal Recollections of John M. Palmer: The Story of an Earnest Life*. Cincinnati, OH: Robert Clarke Company, 1901.

Portrait and Biographical Record of Macoupin County, Illinois. Chicago: Biographical Publishing Company, 1891.

Portraits and Biographical Record of Madison County, Illinois—Containing Biographical Sketches of Prominent and Representative Citizens of the County, Together with Biographies and Portraits of all the Presidents of the United States. Chicago: Biographical Publishing Company, 1894.

Ranken, Jeff. "Marion Morrison: MC's John Wayne Connection." February 12, 2013. http://blogs.monm.edu/archives/2013/02/12/marion-morrison-mcs-john-wayne-connection.

Roady, Charlotte. "His Heart Is Still There." Letter to the editor. *Alton (IL) Telegraph*, August 15, 1975.

Schreier, Philip. "Springfield vs. Enfield." National Rifle Association Museums. http://www.nramuseum.org/media/940660/springfield-enfield.pdf.

Shetley, Paul W. *The Bloody Ninth: A Chronicle of Ninth Illinois*. N.p.: self-published, 2022.

Shiloh National Military Park. "Shiloh Veteran Survives Civil War but Dies in Industrial Accident." Facebook, July 9, 2021. https://www.facebook.com/ShilohNMP/posts/4207181879371766.

Smith, Bethania Meradith. "Civil War Subversives." *Journal of the Illinois State Historical Society* 45, no. 3 (Autumn 1952).

Stanton, Carl. *Macoupin Goes to War: An Account of South Macoupin County Soldiers During and After the Civil War*. N.p.: self-published, January 2001.

Starr, Stephen Z. "Was There a Northwest Conspiracy?" *Filson Club History Quarterly* 38 (1964).

Stillwell, Leander. *The Story of a Common Soldier of Army Life in the Civil War, 1861–1865*. Print on demand. Originally published circa 1920 by Franklin Hudson.

"Unearths Hoard of Old Coins in Jersey County." *Alton (IL) Evening Telegraph*, May 25, 1939.

United States Senate. "The Civil War: The Senate's Story." https://www.senate.gov/artandhistory/history/common/civil_war/VictoryTragedyReconstruction.htm.

Weber, Jennifer L. *Copperheads: The Rise and Fall of Lincoln's Opponents in the North*. New York: Oxford University Press, 2006.

Weeks, Joseph H. "Remembering Andersonville Prison." *Alton Evening Telegraph*, December 16, 1886.

Wilderman, A.S., and A.A. Wilderman, eds. *Historical Encyclopedia of Illinois and History of St. Clair County*. Vol. 1. Chicago: Munsell Publishing Company, 1907.

———. "Memorial to Be Dedicated to Confederate Soldier Sunday." *Telegraph* (Alton, IL), September 30, 2000.

———. "Soldier Gets Gravestone." *Telegraph* (Alton, IL), September 17, 2000.

Word Histories. "To Go to Hell—Or to Heaven—In a Handbasket." March 23, 2018. https://wordhistories.net/2018/05/23/hell-heaven-handbasket.

Works by the Author

"Alton Doctor Could Be Either Healer or Killer." *Telegraph* (Alton, IL), September 25–26 2021.

"Alton Soldier Made Emancipation Real for Slave Owner." *Telegraph* (Alton, IL), September 4–5, 2021.

"Celebrating Spring While Fighting a War." *Telegraph* (Alton, IL), May 8, 2021.

"A Civil War Soldier's Memoir." *St. Louis Post-Dispatch* online edition, December 16, 2015.

"The Drummer Boy of Shiloh." *Springhouse* 29, no. 5.

"The Drummer Boy of Shiloh." *Telegraph* (Alton, IL), July 8, 2012.

"Elsah." *Detours* 7, no. 2 (Summer 2003).

"Elsah." *Illinois* 26, no. 6 (November–December 1987).

"Elsah: Past and Present." *Springhouse* 21, nos. 1–3.

"Former Enemies Who Became Friends." *Medium*, posted September 30, 2022.

"Franklin Moore: Union Cavalryman." *Telegraph* (Alton, IL), May 13, 2012. Revised, expanded version published in *Springhouse* 29, no. 3.

"An Immigrant Who Received the Medal of Honor." *Telegraph* (Alton, IL), January 30, 2019.

"Local Union Veteran Befriended a Confederate." *Telegraph* (Alton, IL), September 17–18, 2022.

"Macoupin Abolitionist Became Confederate General." *Telegraph* (Alton, IL), September 10–11, 2022.

"Shurtleff Grad Freed Kentucky Slaves." *Telegraph* (Alton, IL), September 4, 2011.

"Two Prominent Graduates of Shurtleff College." *Springhouse* 29, no. 1 (n.d.).

"Union Soldiers Used Items from Confederate Homes." *Telegraph* (Alton, IL), October 2–3, 2021.

"An Upper Alton Soldier in Andersonville." *Telegraph* (Alton, IL), October 28, 2012. Later reprinted in a revised, expanded version in *Springhouse* 30, no. 1 (n.d.).

ABOUT THE AUTHOR

John J. Dunphy is the author of three other books for Arcadia/The History Press: *From Christmas to Twelfth Night in Southern Illinois*, *Abolitionism and the Civil War in Southwestern Illinois* and *Murder and Mayhem in Southwestern Illinois*. He owns the Second Reading Book Shop in Alton, Illinois. Visit him on Facebook.

Visit us at
www.historypress.com
....